D1064289

Includes the Latest
Revisions to the Standards

THE
ISO
9000
BOOK

A GLOBAL COMPETITOR'S GUIDE TO COMPLIANCE & CERTIFICATION

SECOND EDITION

**JOHN T. RABBITT
PETER A. BERGH**

QUALITY RESOURCES®
A Division of The Kraus Organization Limited
White Plains, New York

TS
156
.R25
1994

Most Quality Resources books are available at quantity discounts when purchased in bulk. For more information contact:

Special Sales Department
Quality Resources
A Division of The Kraus Organization Limited
902 Broadway
New York, NY 10010

800-247-8519   914-761-9600

Copyright © 1994   John T. Rabbitt and Peter A. Bergh

All rights reserved. No part of this work covered by the copyrights hereon may be reproduced or used in any form or by any means — graphic, electronic, or mechanical, including photocopying, recording, taping, or information storage and retrieval systems — without written permission of the publisher.

Printed in the United States of America

98 97 96 95   10 9 8 7 6 5 4

Quality Resources
A Division of The Kraus Organization Limited
One Water Street
White Plains, NY 10601
914-761-9600
800-247-8519

This book is also distributed by:

AMACOM Books, a division of
American Management Association
135 West 50th Street
New York, NY 10020

The paper used in this publication meets the minimum requirements of the American National Standard for Information Sciences — Permanence of Paper for Printed Library Materials, ANSI Z39.48-1984.

ISBN 0-527-76258-X (Quality Resources)
ISBN 0-8144-0267-4 (AMACOM Books)

Library of Congress Cataloging–in–Publication Data

Rabbitt, John T.
    The ISO 9000 book : a global competitor's guide to compliance and
certification / John T. Rabbitt & Peter A. Bergh. — 2nd ed.
        p.   cm.
    Includes index.
    ISBN 0-527-76258-X (Quality Resources : acid-free). — ISBN 0-8144-0267-4
(AMACOM : acid-free)
    1. Quality control — Standards. 2. Manufactures — Quality control — Standards.
3. Total quality management. I. Bergh, Peter A. II. Title
TS156.R25 1994   94-15521
658.5'62'0218 — dc20   CIP

LONGWOOD COLLEGE LIBRARY
FARMVILLE, VIRGINIA 23901

Dedication

To the employees of The Foxboro Company whose dedication to creating a World Class Enterprise enabled this story to be told.

And, to our wives, Charlotte and Deborah, our children, Beth, Ciara, and Emelie, and our families for their tremendous patience and encouragement throughout the duration of this project.

Contents

Appendix 1 – Are You Ready? 145

Appendix 2 – Sample Quality Manual 169

Preface

The "good old days" are gone. Your customers are changing in response to new global competitive pressures. Some of your customers might already have asked you about the ISO 9000 series quality standards and your intentions in this regard. You are not alone. No matter what business you are in, you will eventually be asked, "Are you ISO certified?" In the U. K., just about every business, from the large multinationals to the local rubbish collector, has pursued or is pursuing certification. These companies recognize that the certification mark will mean more business or, at minimum, survival. It is estimated by an ISO 9000 certification agency that, in the U. S. alone, more than 500,000 operations will eventually seek certification.

Possibly, your experience with today's competitive reality has led you to pick up this book. The more you read about ISO 9000, the more you begin to realize that it is not rocket science. The standard's vagueness, however, can be unnerving as you search for specifics. The reality is that only *you* can interpret the requirements as they relate to your business. It is a common misunderstanding that ISO 9000 is about doing what you say you do and documenting it period. This is only partially correct. You need to ensure that you really *do* what you claim you do, all the time, and that you have addressed some specific requirements as well. There is no single method for meeting ISO 9000 requirements; nor is there a single manual you can buy that will ensure certification. You are the only one who can bring your organization into compliance, and it is our hope that this book will help you get there with a minimum of pain.

This second edition is based on the 1994 revision of the standard, ISO 9000-1-1994. Our intention is to provide you with a working understanding of ISO 9000, its requirements, and methodologies for compliance. We have drawn upon our team experiences at The Foxboro Company, one of the first major U.S. manufacturers to achieve ISO 9001 certification. We hope that the examples of the types of questions that you might encounter when the auditors visit you and the sample quality manual will help jump-start your efforts.

This book is not just about ISO 9000 certification: it is also about creating a sound business, one that will satisfy your customers. ISO 9000 is one of the tools you can use in your TQM journey. The certificate is a "seal of approval" that makes your customers feel better when they do business with you. Ultimately, this book is about improving your bottom line. Whether you are a Fortune 500 manufacturer, a local car dealership, or grocery store, we believe that ISO 9000 will have a positive affect on you. The choice to pursue certification is yours. We hope this book will help you assess the relevance of the standard to your operation and help you achieve certification should you decide to pursue it.

With the 1994 revision, the ISO 9000 standard, is now known as ISO 9000-1. Throughout the book, the use of "ISO 9000" refers to the new standard, ISO 9000-1.

1

How Did We Get Here?

ISO 9000 is more than just a standard. It reflects a well-organized operation with trained and motivated people. It is the new challenge. Those who move quickly will enjoy the fruits that result from being a leader. Those who defer will feel the pain of lost business. But beyond that, it's about running your business guided by common-sense principles that have existed for most of this century.

To put ISO 9000 in its proper perspective, it is useful to examine the evolution of manufacturing. The following is a nonacademic perspective.

From Farm to Factory

The first "manufactured" products were relatively simple, and a single craftsman would assemble and test the complete product. Usually, the craftsman was the only supplier in town for his specific product. His customers knew where he lived, he made house calls, and the entire village knew his family history. Times were great if you didn't mind ill-fitting, expensive, and hard-to-get material goods. It was just a matter of time before someone would realize that if all the craftsmen were moved into a single location, more could be produced at reduced costs.

A short time later, Samuel Slater arrived from England and started the first U.S. textile mill in Rhode Island. Since then nothing has been the same. Slater learned the secret of building machines for specific tasks and the use of low-cost farm labor to run them. Soon, all over New England's fast moving streams, those tiny mills became brick textile monoliths producing good, inexpensive textile goods.

Just as mass production was being born, Fred Taylor discovered that breaking tasks down into smaller elements, providing specific tools, and linking them closely would result in increased production. The United States was in a very rapid growth stage and experienced unprecedented demand for its cheap goods. Wave after wave of mostly non-English speaking and untrained immigrants flowed into the work force. Industry at that time was new and its leaders saw no alternative to Taylorism. The new industries as well as the nation grew from this base of low-cost, low-skilled labor.

As organizations grew, planning was split off from the production function it was meant to serve. Walls were erected to reduce the noise for the accountants and planners. Later those walls turned into offices with doors. New products were being designed in locations away from the production process, which made communications more difficult. With an overwhelming demand for goods, sins of waste and poor quality were quickly forgiven as new and less expensive products rolled out to meet an insatiable demand.

Enlightened Manufacturing

Much earlier in this century, the visionary, Henry Ford, saw a different way of conducting business. He expounded on the ideas of continuous improvement and waste reduction. In his book, *Today and Tomorrow*, written in 1926, he discusses how the concepts of process and linked flows were introduced and practiced. Ford drove his organization to continually look at the entire process and to continually work to improve each step. He knew his business and insisted that his employees do the same.

Ford felt that his employees and customers were one and the same, and unless an organization took care of its employees, it would destroy itself. He also believed that satisfying his customers was the greatest service he could provide, that satisfaction came from a continually lower cost of ownership, and that the world belonged to those who provided this service.

In 1908, the first Model T was introduced at a material cost of $850 and by 1924 he had not only dramatically improved the reliability of the vehicle, but had driven the material costs down to $290. Ford finished production of the Model T in 1927 and had sold more than 15,000,000 units.

Ford also pioneered the concepts of Process Integrity, Total Quality Control, Just In Time (JIT) and Kanban feed systems. He never allowed more than one shift's worth of material on the assembly floor. "Our production cycle is about eighty-one hours from the mine to the finished machine in the freight car." Today, that is about how long it takes to move the average material through incoming inspection. Ford also established the concepts of waste of inventory, energy conservation, employee training, employee safety, and cleanliness on the job site.

When asked to give advice to someone starting out (and the reason for his success), Ford said, "If we do that which is before us to do in the best way that we know, that is, if we faithfully try to serve, we do not have to worry about anything else. The future has a way of taking care of itself."

The Boom Years

After Ford created his eighth wonder of the world, bankers and stockbrokers began the process of speculation and uncontrolled borrowing. Meanwhile, the public adopted the Roaring '20s mind-set of "live for today." This nonproductive activity eventually caused the collapse of the capital market and drove the country into the depression of the 1930s.

For the next 10 years people lived conservatively. As World War II created a new demand for goods as well as shortages, the U.S. economy began to recover. The government created war-related jobs and rationed consumer goods to keep inflation down while participating in the destruction of a large segment of the world's industrial capacity. By the end of World War II, the U.S. had enjoyed four years of full employment. However, the little opportunity for consumer spending created an enormous capital base and a high demand for consumer goods. In addition, the troops came home and started buying goods from our intact U.S. factories at an unprecedented rate. The U.S. government then lent money to selected, war-ravaged countries to buy goods from the only remaining intact industry base, which was the U.S.

This resulted in an unparalleled shortage of goods. New inexperienced manufacturers emerged as a result of the shortages and product quality continued to decline. For example the Kaiser-Frazer auto company was founded when a liberty ship builder teamed up with Joseph Frazer, a very successful car salesman from Packard and General Motors. They really didn't know anything about building cars, but that didn't stop them. Although the car they developed did have some innovative features, they still had not overcome technical issues such as hard steering, gear whine, and wheel shimmy. However, when the car was introduced, it sold as if there was no tomorrow. Demand subsided in the early 1950s, marking the demise of Kaiser-Frazer. The motto of the 1950s and 1960s was "Make the Schedule." This worked quite nicely for the U.S. economy as it grew at an extraordinary rate. Then in the mid-1960s, German "bugs" started popping up everywhere, followed by a series of Japanese "beetles."

The Japanese Listened

Japan's industrial base was destroyed by the end of World War II. The country was occupied, and its consumers were broke and out of work. Japan had no where to go but up. It actually employed a recovery strategy that typifies most growing nations, and there are clear transition points. In the 1950s, Japan focused on low-cost, labor-intensive, low-technology industries like textiles. Meanwhile, U.S. quality gurus Deming and Juran were teaching lessons on process control and management throughout Japan.

During the 1960s, the Japanese had amassed enough capital to engage in a "Large Scale Manufacturing" based strategy that focused on productivity improvements. During the 1970s they developed flexible manufacturing strategies that incorporated both the "Scales" strategy with the

"Variety" approach. Meanwhile, cheap labor was becoming a thing of the past. Japanese industry was moving beyond Ford's concepts into new frontiers. Concurrently, the U.S. was becoming infatuated with computers and their promise of effortless salvation.

> **"Listen to me, and in five years you**
> **will be competing with the West.**
> **Keep listening, and soon the West will**
> **be demanding protection from you."**
> *W. Edwards Deming, speaking to 45 key*
> *Japanese industrialists at a seminar in 1950*

American industry believed the computer salvation story until the late 1980s. Ironically, during the early 1980s, the computer industry was already in the process of replacing massive computer-driven shop floor control systems with JIT and Kanban, but they weren't telling, lest they shoot the golden goose. In fact, a computer-industry pioneer was told not to make a speech at an industrial conference on JIT for fear of damaging the industry. The U.S. was losing the race, and it wasn't until the late 1970s that the lessons learned by the Japanese started beating the daylights out of our industries. The weak players were the first to feel the impact.

The Declining Years

In 1979, the Ford Motor Company recalled more cars than it produced. In consumers' eyes, "Ford" became an acronym for "Fix or Repair Daily" and Ford's customers were getting a "Better Idea" from the competition. The effect on the business was devastating, thousands were laid off, and industry observers were wondering if they were witnessing the demise of the Founding Father of the automotive industry. Meanwhile, our consumer electronics industry was rapidly migrating offshore. According to U.S. Labor Department statistics, during the mid-1980s, many new jobs were created, giving the illusion that the economy was on an even keel. But these were low-wage service sector jobs, and the U.S. was losing 20,000 to 30,000 manufacturing jobs a month to foreign manufacturing.

In 1980, Ford executives asked Dr. Deming to come in and breathe some life into their failing entity. Dr. Deming gave them some very sound advice that began with knowing their process and gaining stability within their operation. By the mid-1980s, the Japanese were evolving their "Variety and Speed" strategy. General Motors (GM) had determined that they would automate out of existence the very thing that Ford had considered his most valuable asset — people. GM made a big bet on strategies such as MAP (manufacturing automation protocol) as the answer to this latest competitive challenge, even though there was clear evidence that the organizations that were beating them in the marketplace were employing a different approach.

> **"You can always count on the**
> **Americans to do the right thing!**
> **...but, only after they have tried everything else..."**
> *Winston Churchill*

By 1985, Ford had achieved a remarkable rebound and had just out-earned GM. By 1987, Ford boosted profits by an additional 40%. What caused this remarkable turnaround? Ford gained control of its processes and met a minimum set of *customer expectations*, which is the essence of ISO 9000.

It's About More Than Just ISO 9000

Currently, the Europeans are banding together to create the world's largest market with new barriers. The Asian basin is afire with development and growth. Awareness and recognition are growing for the need to rethink how we run our businesses — to refocus on elimination of nonvalue-adding functions and to put the customer above all else. The emergence and growing global acceptance of ISO 9000 conveniently provides a framework for businesses to assess where they are and where they want to be. In addition, conformance to the standard demonstrates a minimum level of acceptable performance that is universally recognized and accepted. The following chapters will describe how the pursuit of ISO 9000 is simply good business practice.

2

Why All The Fuss?

The ISO 9000 standards represent the common denominator of business quality that is accepted internationally. In 1987 they were adopted by the International Organization for Standardization (ISO). ISO 9000 certification demonstrates the capability of a supplier to control the processes that determine the acceptability of the product or service being supplied.

By mid-1993, more than 30,000 European companies had been certified and the numbers continue to grow dramatically. North American companies were initially slow to recognize the importance of achieving certification. The situation has since changed significantly, and by the end of 1993, more than 2,000 North American operations had been certified. According to Quality Systems Update, we have now entered a period of geometric growth in the number of operations achieving certification. While certification to the standard is not mandatory in the EU (European Union), formerly the EEC (European Economic Community) and more recently the EC (European Community), one can expect that when a certified supplier is competing with a noncertified supplier, the certified one will be preferred.

The Basics

ISO 9000 is a foundation for running a business well. Just as different types of structures require different foundations, so do different businesses. Thus, the standards to which a company can be registered, ISO 9001 through ISO 9003 apply to enterprises according to the scope of their activities. ISO 9004 and the ISO 9000-X family are documents that provide specific guidelines for specific industrial applications, as seen in Figure 2.1.

Of the three ISO 9000 standards, ISO 9001 is the most comprehensive in scope, confirming process conformance from the initial development of a product through production, test, installation, and servicing. ISO 9002 covers only the procurement, production, installation and servicing portion of your business. Both standards require the same degree of conformance to their respective scope of activity. For example, when comparing two suppliers of a commodity item, such as paper, if one has ISO 9001 certification and the other has ISO 9002 certification, it does not mean that the ISO 9001 operation has a better process. However, if you require the producer to provide design work for you, then the ISO 9001 certified supplier is the supplier of choice, as ISO 9002 does not provide for a review of this area.

ISO 9003, unlike the previous two, addresses only final inspection and testing and has a significantly lower conformance requirement. This standard is somewhat controversial and many feel that it generally undermines the entire standard especially when a company uses it solely to claim certification. Figure 2.2 shows the relationships among the three standards.

As you work your way through the standard, you may find yourself asking, "What do they really mean?" The truth is that it is intentionally vague in certain ways, so it can accommodate just about any business operation. Recognizing this, the standard is devised so that you can meet its basic requirements by operating your business your way. ISO 9000 defines basic principles for a sound business operation and you must interpret it according to your business. You are the expert, and only you can define how you operate. ISO 9000 requires that you simply operate in the manner that you say you do while meeting certain basic requirements. This is not rocket science by any stretch.

There is a great deal of misinformation about the standard in the business community. In 1992, approximately 300 sites in the U.S. had been certified, yet more than 5,000 consultants claimed ISO 9000 expertise — this just didn't make sense. The number of consultants

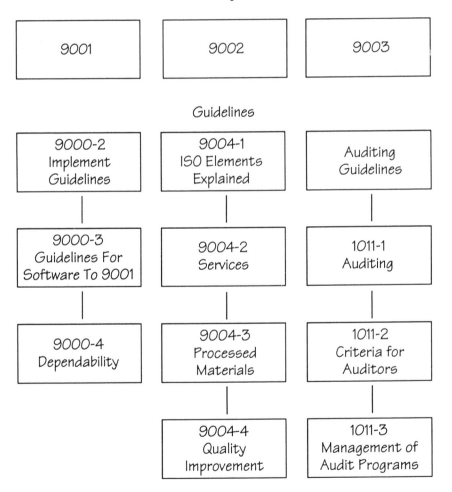

Figure 2.1 The ISO 9000 family of standards and guidelines.

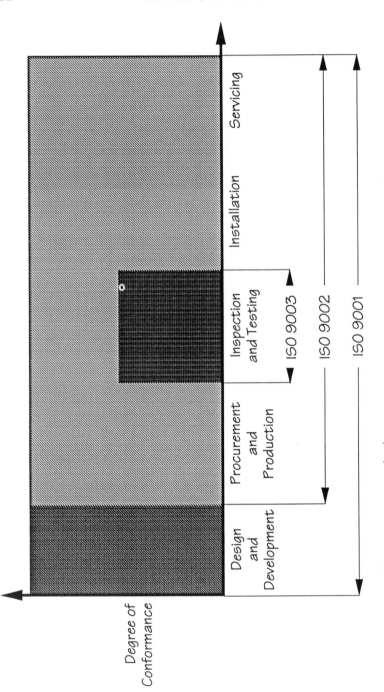

Figure 2.2 Scope of the ISO 9000 standards.
Source: Det Norske Veritas.

continues to exceed the number of certified sites. On the other hand, although you can't buy certification through a consultant, the best ones can be very helpful in advising you and seeing you through the process.

The 20 Elements

The ISO 9000 standard focuses on 20 aspects of a quality program that are subject to a rigorous audit during the certification process. Each section relates to a specific aspect of satisfying customers. When trying to determine how each section applies to your organization, ask yourself how it relates to your customer's expectations. The following 20 elements are contained in Section 4 of the ISO 9000 standard document.

4.1 • Management responsibility
4.2 • Quality system
4.3 • Contract review
4.4 • Design control
4.5 • Document and data control
4.6 • Purchasing
4.7 • Control of customer supplied product
4.8 • Product identification and traceability
4.9 • Process control
4.10 • Inspection and testing
4.11 • Control of inspection, measuring, and test equipment
4.12 • Inspection and test status
4.13 • Control of nonconforming product
4.14 • Corrective and preventive action
4.15 • Handling, storage, packaging, preservation, and delivery
4.16 • Control of quality records
4.17 • Internal quality audits
4.18 • Training
4.19 • Servicing
4.20 • Statistical techniques

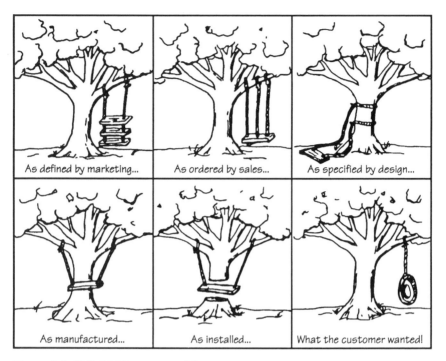

Figure 2.3 ISO 9000 prevents this.

The Customer's Perspective

The following is a brief explanation of each element of the standard from a customer's perspective.

4.1 • Management responsibility – Who is responsible for ensuring that the product or service is what I ordered and when? Who ensures that your system is effectively managed?

4.2 • Quality system – Is the quality system in place to ensure that everything delivered to me is as you said it would be? How do you make sure?

4.3 • Contract review – What is your system for ensuring that what marketing and sales sold me is actually what I will be getting and when?

4.4 • *Design control* – Show me how you designed the product and how you ensure it does what you say it does. Is there agreement between the designers and salespeople that it works as they claim? If you make changes to the design, how is it determined that my product is still acceptable?

4.5 • *Document and data control* – How do you inform manufacturing of the requirements and materials for building the product? If you make a change to the requirements, how is that communicated? If I need parts, will you be able to tell me what to order? If changes are made in the material requirements, how is manufacturing informed of how to test it or when to acquire the new parts? Will the service organization know which parts are needed for a repair job?

4.6 • *Purchasing* – Can you show me how you are making sure that your purchasing group is buying what your designers and engineers are specifying? How do you know you are buying from a supplier who makes good product and delivers it on time?

4.7 • *Control of customer supplied product* – When I send you my materials, show me how you protect, store, and maintain them. If there is a problem with the materials, show us how you will remedy it.

4.8 • *Product identification and traceability* – Show me how you ensure the materials don't get mixed up with others and that they are really what you ordered. How do you check that they are what the drawings say they are? How do you ensure the correct materials are used when building my product?

4.9 • *Process control* – Show me that you have procedures in place to build my product properly — I'm especially concerned with procedures on critical items relative to the manufacture of my product. Do you know how to make my product correctly and can you distinguish between the right way and the wrong way? Do you know when you are making junk? Do you have any points in the process where you cannot tell by inspection that the product is acceptable? How do you handle this? They should be written down so people can easily access them if they have any questions or if they want to train someone.

4.10 • *Inspection and testing* – How do you ensure that I will receive what I ordered? Have you verified that my product will work as promised? I mean really tested — can you show me?

4.11 • *Control of inspection, measuring and test equipment* – How do you ensure that the equipment you are using to test the correctness of my product is accurate? How are you doing this?

4.12 • *Inspection and test status* – Show me how it is indicated on my product that it was tested.

4.13 • *Control of nonconforming product* – When it is discovered that part of my product doesn't work or fit as it should, is there an established procedure for fixing it? Does everyone know what to do when it is fixed? I would like it to be retested. How do you know it didn't get mixed in with other products after you discovered it wasn't correct?

4.14 • *Corrective and preventive action* – If you find a problem with a product or if a customer complains, what is the procedure for ensuring it doesn't happen again? Are you writing new procedures and training people to ensure it doesn't occur again?

4.15 • *Handling, storage, packaging, preservation, and delivery* – How are you ensuring my product was built properly and that it is packaged, preserved, and stored to prevent damage? Can you make sure the delivery process keeps my product from being damaged?

4.16 • *Control of quality records* – Do you have procedures to document the quality of my product? This should include the raw materials records. Could I find these records quickly if that was our agreement?

4.17 • *Internal quality audits* – How do you ensure that you are running your operation as you claim? Have you trained a group of people to review your operation? Can you show me records that demonstrate that attention has been given to the critical areas? Can you show me where the management in the area has fixed a problem discovered by the audit team?

4.18 • *Training* – Prove to me that the people who built and tested my product are trained. Do they know all the critical aspects of my product and how it should work? Has the supervisor agreed that the person is trained properly?

4.19 • *Servicing* – If you told me you could service my product, how would you do that? Can you ensure that you will conduct your operations as well as you did when you first built my product (i.e., good parts, delivered on time, tested again)? Can you ensure that my product will be worked on only by someone who has been properly trained?

4.20 • *Statistical techniques* – If you are using statistical techniques to validate that my product is good, could you show me that they work? Does everyone who is using these techniques know what to do when it is indicated that the process is out of control or moving outside the control limits?

Hopefully, this brief look at ISO 9000 from a customer's perspective provides a working approach to the standard. To avoid confusion, just keep asking yourself, what does my customer want?

ISO 9000 — An Everyday Example

One example that demonstrates how ISO 9000 applies to an everyday situation is having the brakes of your car worked on at the local garage. You remember a local garage's ad for a special on brake repairs; in addition, you recall a neighbor speaking highly of the place.

As you approach the front counter of the shop, your journey through ISO 9000 begins. The clerk listens to your experience with the brakes as well as about your car. He informs you that your car will require metallic brake pads that will cost extra. You agree to go ahead with the job and the clerk promises your car will be ready in one hour.

As you wait, you mull over your main concerns: Will the car stop properly? Will the repair cost more than was stated? Will they complete the work in an hour? This is what ISO 9000 is all about — confidence that the task will be done *as promised.* The ISO 9000 standard encompasses many details that would easily be taken for granted. As illustrated in the rest of this example, the standard requires that attention be paid to every aspect of the brake job.

You realize that when you picked up the advertisement, there was a management structure that made sure the business ran well and that quality methods and practices are used, which gave the garage a good reputation. You want to be confident that the mechanic knows where to get the work order papers for your car, and actually gets *your* car. Hopefully the mechanic has been trained to drive your car onto the ramp properly, disassemble the brakes, and inspect them to ensure nothing else is wrong. Then that the mechanic goes to the proper documents and determines which brake shoes are right for your car and retrieves the parts from a bin with the shoes correctly identified. You would expect that if a mechanic tried to use some parts that ended up not fitting, he would have removed them from stock rather than putting them back in and passing the problem on to someone else. You hope that this person can assemble the brakes to the proper torque requirements and finally test them by driving your car around the block. You expect to be provided with a check sheet of the items tested and that your car was parked in a safe place. This section with the mechanic covers many of the twenty ISO 9000 elements.

4.1 • Management responsibility – Someone is in control ensuring that the organization is selling products and services in the fashion it claims to.

4.2 • Quality system – The owners of the operation have a quality system in place to ensure their business operates as indicated. When you approached the counter, the clerk created a contract with you. This person was knowledgeable about the product and communicated with the shop to know approximately how long it would be. The clerk had the training and documents to know that your car required metallic pads, where you should leave your car, and what to do when you returned to pick it up. This person was also willing and able to address your further questions and concerns.

4.3 • Contract review – Ensures that the work performed by the mechanic was what you had agreed to with the clerk.

4.4 • *Design control* – Ensures that the brakes placed on your car were properly designed, tested, and documented so as to perform the job as specified.

4.5 • *Document and data control* – Ensures that the documents and reference books were available to the mechanic for the proper selection of materials and the appropriate testing.

4.6 • *Purchasing* – Ensures that the mechanic had the correct parts available.

4.8 • *Product identification and traceability* – Ensures that the brake linings retrieved from the stock bin were marked properly.

4.9 • *Process control* – There were established procedures for the mechanic to do the job, fill out the paperwork, find information on the materials, and access usable assembly instructions.

4.10 • *Inspection and testing* – The mechanic did some form of inspection and test to ensure that your new brakes were acting properly.

4.11 • *Control of inspection, measuring, and test equipment* – Ensures that the testing and measurement setting devices are calibrated to the correct torques and the right tools are being used to do it.

4.12 • *Inspection and test status* – Ensures that the check-off sheet is a working document and that tests were performed.

4.13 • *Control of nonconforming product* – Ensures that the mechanic knows what to do if a possible problem is detected with the material and how it should be treated and identified to prevent it from ending up on the other side of your car.

4.14 • *Corrective and preventive action* – Ensures that the mechanic and his management have a procedure for fixing known problems.

4.15 • *Handling, storage, packaging, preservation, and delivery* – The mechanic must know how to handle the brake pads before installation and ensure that they have been stored in a protected area. In addition, the mechanic must know where to put your car, keys and paperwork when completed.

4.16 • *Control of quality records* – The mechanic fills out a standard checklist, makes additional notes on the procedure being performed, and perhaps even has a place to record related issues for you to consider and for the shop to note.

4.17 • *Internal quality audits* – The supervisor should be regularly observing the areas to ensure that the mechanic has all the correct materials and documents and is performing tasks correctly.

4.18 • *Training* – This ensures that the mechanic had the proper training before working on your car and that the supervisor went over the task and verified that the mechanic was successful in all aspects of the job.

4.19 • *Servicing* – Ensures that the mechanic knows what to do if something doesn't work correctly with the new brakes.

4.20 • *Statistical techniques* – This ensures that metrics are kept regarding the quality of the service provided at the garage and are reviewed to ensure that the processes remain in control and that problem areas are quickly identified.

You notice an hour has passed. You go to the front desk. The clerk says, "Your car is coming out right now and we noticed that your driver's side windshield wiper was worn, so we replaced it free of charge, as our management believes your safety is paramount. Here are your keys and an itemized check sheet of all the tasks completed. This will also act as your warranty. Please note our toll-free number should you have any problems or wish to make an appointment for any of your other vehicles. Thank you for your patronage and please drive carefully."

ISO 9000 alone didn't create customer satisfaction, but it was a foundation on which to build...

That's what all the fuss is about!

This is a simple tale about brakes being fixed and a very happy customer in the end. It illustrated an ISO 9000 compliant organization taking care of the customer in a way that met the customer's expectations. However, it wasn't conformance to the ISO 9000 standard alone that made the customer pleased with having the brakes fixed. It was that extra touch of the 75¢ wiper being put on the car that showed that they cared. This was later reinforced when the clerk mentioned to drive carefully. By providing the customer with a special toll-free telephone number, the garage reinforced that it valued the business. These extra little items all exceeded his expectations, and the checklist reaffirmed the expectation of good value for the expected task. When you combine performance of the primary task to a normal expectation (ISO 9000 defined), and then go beyond that expectation, you end up with a very happy customer. That's what quality is all about — creating customer satisfaction.

ISO 9000, Quality, and the Baldrige

Although ISO 9000 certification can provide your customer with a degree of comfort and confidence about your process and your ability to deliver the product as promised, it also provides your organization with the ability to reduce costs, improve delivery, and increase speed. As seen with the brakes example, ISO 9000 does not perform these modern day miracles by itself, but works within an overall quality model.

Renowned quality experts Deming, Juran, and Crosby have each promoted a set of 10-14 steps or points that they believe address the issue of quality. All these points or steps are valid and they share some common threads. We took the liberty of boiling them down to the seven critical ones listed below. Note that the first three positions are occupied by elements of ISO 9000.

The Seven Business Quality Success Factors

1. **Customer focus**
2. **Process versus results focus**
3. **Management commitment/responsibility**
4. **Continuous improvement**
5. **Less than 20% of problems caused by workers**
6. **Performance measures**
7. **Cross functional councils create constancy**

A company's position in the quality evolution is indicated by its level of employee involvement and market presence. ISO 9000 is at the very basic end of the quality evolution and provides you with stability and the minimum attributes for market survival, as shown in Figure 2.4. With ISO 9000 compliance and certification you will notice increased employee involvement and the ability to more easily correct problems, as we will describe in the following chapter.

ISO 9000 vs. The Baldrige

The following are some commonly asked questions related to ISO 9000 and the Malcolm Baldrige National Quality Award.

1 • Should we go for the Baldrige or ISO 9000 certification first?

Go for ISO 9000 compliance first. Achieving certification will help you prepare for the Baldrige. The 1992 applications for the Baldrige Award were down, and it was the feeling of the Baldrige committee that this was in response to companies going for ISO 9000 certification first.

2 • What's the difference between ISO 9000 and the Baldrige Award?

ISO focuses very closely on your internal processes, especially manufacturing, sales, administration, and technical support and services. The Baldrige places more emphasis on customer satisfaction and business results. The differences between the two are illustrated in Figure 2.5 and Figure 2.6. ISO 9000 is an elemental tool while the Baldrige looks at how many tools are integrated into a cohesive program that results in customer satisfaction and business results.

3 • Do you have to be ISO 9000 certified before going for the Baldrige?

The Baldrige assumes you have your processes under control and, therefore, awards relatively few points in this area. The Baldrige addresses the issues of customer satisfaction, business results, and the competitive aspects of gaining increased sales and profitability. ISO 9000 virtually ignores competitive positioning or business results.

ISO 9000 vs. The Shingo Prize

The Shingo Prize is another award (tool) that has been growing in popularity. It was established in 1988 and is administered by the Utah State University, College of Business at Logan. The award is given annually to manufacturers who exhibit world class manufacturing leadership. The sections of the Shingo Prize requirements relative to ISO 9000 are illustrated in Figure 2.7.

Like the Baldrige, the Shingo Prize requirements assume that your processes are under control. The Shingo, however, places a high emphasis on productivity improvements. It is projected that as manufacturers reach comparable levels of quality, productivity (cost reduction) will become an even greater differentiator.

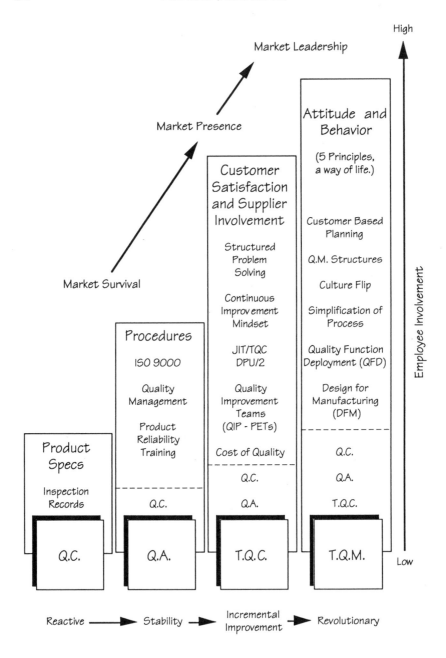

Figure 2.4 ISO 9000 is at the very basic end of the quality evolution, providing stability and the minimum attributes for market survival.

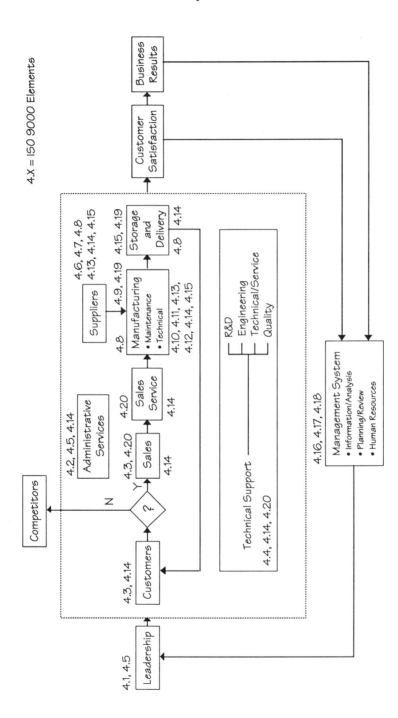

Figure 2.5 ISO 9000 vs. the Baldrige — ISO 9000 emphasis areas.
Source: Weyerhaeuser Company.

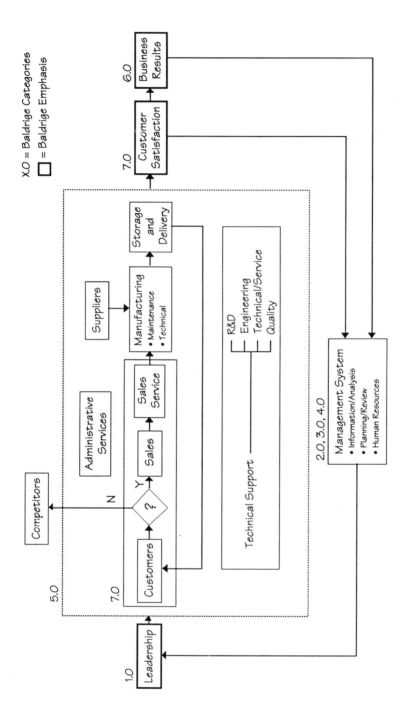

Figure 2.6 ISO 9000 vs. the Baldrige — Baldrige emphasis areas.
Source: Weyerhaeuser Company.

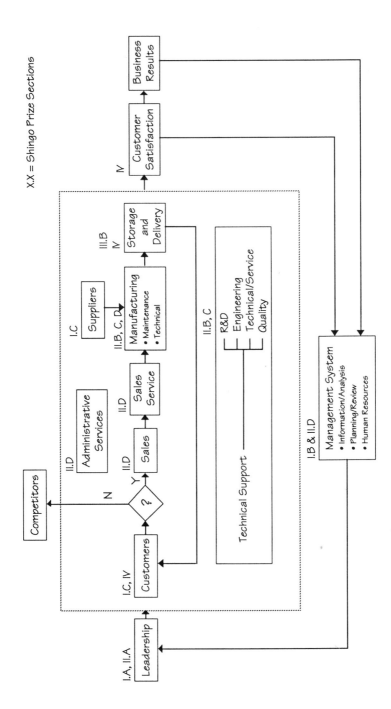

Figure 2.7 ISO 9000 vs. the Shingo Prize — Shingo Prize Sections.
Source: Adapted to chart provided by Weyerhaeuser Company.

3

What If We Don't Do It?

What do the 320 million people of the European Community share?
What standard has every major industrialized nation adopted?
What could contribute to a significant boost to your bottom line?
What have the big three auto manufacturers adopted?
What certification status is now included in your D&B report?
What's being incorporated into U.S. Department of Defense and NATO purchasing requirements?
What is being incorporated into the Good Manufacturing Practices standards?

The answer: ISO 9000.

This chapter will review what ISO 9000 means to your operation and describes why you may be required to comply.

Good Business Sense, Even When Times Are Good

If your profits are up and business prospects look rosy, you may feel no motivation to change your operations. After all, pain is usually what motivates change. You may be leading your market thanks to new technology — but new technology is also soon-to-be-copied technology. It's unlikely that you'll enjoy those margins indefinitely. Success is great, but one of its main dangers is complacency. Now may be an ideal time to dive into the ISO 9000 compliance process. If your firm is experiencing falling sales or profits, then ISO 9000 may be an effective first step for turning the situation around.

The world has changed — in the 1950s and 1960s a business could operate based on the following formula.

$$\text{Product Cost} + \text{Desired Profit} = \text{Sales Price}$$

Within reason, you could name your price, and with the appropriate marketing support, you could derive your desired profit. Product cost was not a primary consideration in design or production, and niche marketing would support your sales price.

The 1990s present an entirely different business climate. Our once attractive formula for business success has been transposed.

$$\text{Sales Price} - \text{Product Cost} = \text{Profit}$$

Today, markets quickly set and drive prices down, and consumers have difficulty differentiating the performance and quality of competing products. Marketing efforts have mostly saturated consumers. Profit is now often a result of how well you can control and reduce your costs,

"No! I can't be bothered to see any crazy salesman.
We've got a battle to fight!"

Figure 3.1

which historically has been a weak link. Business in the 1990s will require you to employ every effort on *total cost reduction*. This means more than a purchase price variance on raw materials. It means reducing costs in administration, design, manufacturing—in every corner of your business. We previously listed some questions that address specific benefits of ISO 9000 certification. We will now examine three broad issues that encompass those specifics:

• European competitiveness.
• Market perception of your company's fitness.
• Internal organizational health.

European Competitiveness

Although it has been endorsed by the EU (formerly the EC), ISO 9000 is not a European conspiracy to lock out foreign products. The ISO 9000 standard actually originated from the quality standards of the U.S. Department of Defense (MIL-Q9858) in the late 1950s. These standards were adopted by the British Standards Institution, and the scope was expanded to incorporate the entire business process and was designated as the British Standard 5750 code in 1979. The International Organization for Standardization adapted the British 5750 code and issued the ISO 9000 standard series in 1987. The first major revision to the standard was issued in 1994 and renamed as ISO 9000-1-1994.

Although ISO 9000 evolved technically in Europe, the International Organization for Standardization consists of members from more than 100 countries. In the early 1990s, an American from AT&T was chairing the group. This is a truly global standard.

What really makes Europe so pivotal in the development of the standard, and what in turn makes the standard so vital to businesses of all nations, is that the European Community has made the standard law. An interesting chain of events has moved the standard into its present European prominence.

During the past 15 years, the European economies have lagged behind those of the U.S. and Japan. The Europeans recognized that trade barriers between their countries have undermined their ability to compete internationally and grow. Some European firms have as many as 12 distinct standards to comply with. Multiple standards discourage manufacturers from trading outside of their own, well-understood, smaller domestic markets, depriving them of the economies of scale that a large international market allows. By eliminating trade barriers, European manufacturers would have access to a $4 trillion market with more than 320 million potential customers. The bordering non-EC countries also recognized the benefits of a common market and the seven European Free Trade Association (EFTA) members petitioned to acquire a special trading arrangement with the EC. They have reached an agreement that means the new European market will consist of 19 countries (states of the EC) and a total of 380 million people. If the countries of the former Soviet block begin petitioning, we could easily witness the formation of a half-billion consumer market.

In June of 1985, the Europeans declared their intentions for barrier-free trade by December 31, 1992. No one expected that this would be anything but a complicated task requiring compromises among the EC member countries unlike any that had preceded them. Since that time, Europe has made significant progress, but many major hurdles remain, which probably won't be completely resolved until the turn of the century. One of these hurdles is the incorporation of a broad set of common standards into legislation. Upon acceptance, each piece of legislation becomes a "Legislated Directive" that can have an impact on any aspect of business within the EC. As the Legislated Directives are generated by the EC, they are then adopted by the member states and placed into national statutes. Only a handful of these directives were in place for 1993.

The European requirements for ISO 9000 product or industry compliance continues to evolve. For starters, the EC has specified classes of products that are either "regulated" or "nonregulated." Regulated products are those that have a health, safety, or environmental impact and are required to be manufactured in compliance with ISO 9000. Examples of regulated products are children's toys, computer terminals, and food packaging.

If you produce a nonregulated product, however, don't assume that ISO 9000 doesn't apply. ISO 9000 is quickly becoming the minimum requirement for doing business, regulated or not! In response to the varying technical standards for regulated products, the EC established the following groups to ensure harmonization among the standards: CEN for nonelectrical requirements (ISO 9000), CENELEC for electrical requirements, and ETSI for telecommunications standards. Figure 3.2 shows the relationship between these groups and the international standards bodies.

The EC has passed a series of general legislative directives and left the details up to groups like CEN to define. It is the purpose of these groups to harmonize the various standards such that all manufacturers could support a common requirement and thus allow free trade among the member states.

CEN adopted the ISO 9000 standards verbatim and renamed them as the EN 29000 series with its corresponding breakdown. CEN recognized that process stability and the robustness of the standard would deliver a better product, thereby, raising the general quality of European products throughout the community. One way to promote this standard was to encourage third-party certification.

> "The Commission has recognized the important role (quality assurance) techniques can play and so will not only promote their usage but will encourage the use of third party certification of quality systems when it is carried out in a transparent manner, inducing mutual recognition throughout the Community. Moreover, the commission considers that such techniques can also be used in legislation, either to enhance the credibility of a manufacturer's declaration or to complement, reduce or bring more flexibility to third party intervention in respect to the products themselves." (EOTC progress report of 1990)

To promote confidence in third-party certification, the EC established the EN 45000 series of standards to qualify testing labs and registrars. As a result, each member nation established a formal recommendation

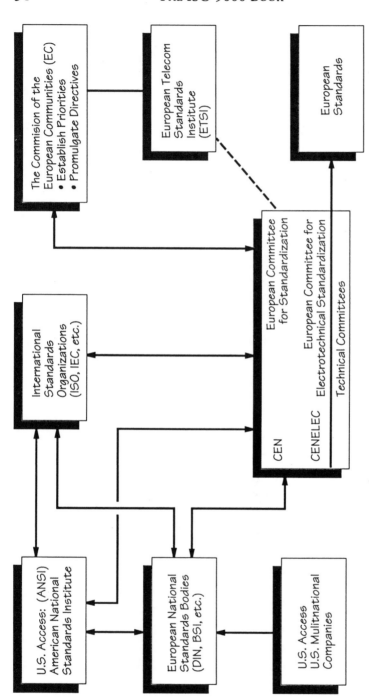

Figure 3.2 Relationship among standards bodies.

board that reports to the government. This board recommends various third-party certification agencies. Examples of these recommending boards are the Raad voor de Certificatie (RvC) of Holland, the National Accreditation Council for Certifying Bodies (NACCB) of the United Kingdom, and the Registrar Accreditation Board (RAB) of the U.S. Once a third-party agency is accepted by the board, it is listed as a *notified body* or *accredited registrar* in the EC product directives. The notified bodies or third-party certification agents can then provide a *recognized registration mark* of the sponsoring governmental agency. For example, the third-party registration firm of Det Norske Veritas (DNV) can provide a registration mark of the RvC (see Figure 3.3) or the NACCB to its customers who have undergone a successful ISO 9000 audit depending on the audit scheme used.

A careful look at all the directives indicates that process quality certification (ISO 9000) by a third party is generally not required. However, the blanket endorsement of the third-party certification process by the EC council and other EC legislative actions makes it a de facto requirement. For example, products sold within the EC will be subject to new legislation related to product liability and safety. The EC product liability directive states that a manufacturer, regardless of fault or negligence, is liable to a person who is harmed by a faulty product. The product safety directive requires manufacturers to monitor the safety of their products throughout the product's lifetime. The result of these two

Figure 3.3 *Registration mark of the RvC issued by third-party registration firm Det Norske Veritas.*

directives is that a manufacturer must document that it has maintained a defect-free manufacturing process. If a manufacturer is required to defend itself in a court and can demonstrate that through its processes and third-party certification that it did produce products in a defect-free environment and met the appropriate EC standards, it may be able to free itself of the liability and enjoy the appropriate liability protection afforded it under EC law. ISO 9000 requires that you've surveyed and carefully selected your suppliers as part of the *purchasing* requirement. For example, if a European manufacturer has four equivalent suppliers, three in Europe certified to ISO 9000 and one noncertified located in the U.S., do you think it would spend $5,000-$10,000 to send a review team to the U.S. just to maintain another supplier? More and more European purchase agreements will require demonstrated compliance to ISO 9000.

Market Perception of Your Company's Fitness

ISO 9000 certification will impact your domestic business in at least the following four areas:

1. Competition against suppliers who are certified.
2. Certified organizations focused on continuous improvement.
3. Media awareness.
4. Customer perception.

Competition Against Suppliers Who Are Certified

Usually, members of a sales force are trained to capitalize on the strengths of their products and organization. They are also made aware of the competitive issues affecting their organization. If you teach your sales people about ISO 9000 certification and explain why you are requiring certification from your suppliers for the parts that go into the products they sell, they will not hesitate to relate this to their customers. You will want to provide a copy of the certificate to each member of the sales team.

You may also want to coach them on how to discuss certification, as the following example illustrates.

In this example, you have two identical toasters, both certified by a reputable laboratory for safety. One toaster is manufactured in an ISO 9000 compliant environment, that is, the designs are correctly replicated to the manufacturing organization, the approved raw materials are purchased, the product is properly assembled by trained employees, tested properly, and packaged and transported according to procedures. The organization can make incremental improvements in the product because of its stable process. The customer has a high probability of receiving the product on time, with a low failure rate, and with an ideal mean-time-between-failure (MTBF).

If the same toaster is built in a noncertified facility, it cannot be demonstrated that its designs have been properly replicated by the manufacturing operations, that purchasing was done from a reliable supplier, or that it has been properly assembled by trained employees. There is nothing to show that it was tested properly or to current specifications. There were no guarantees that it was packaged or transported according to procedure. Given this environment, there is a higher probability of late deliveries, higher initial failure rates, and most likely a lower MTBF. One could easily conclude that the company is probably out of control, otherwise it would have been certified to ISO 9000.

Even though a supplier might have full approval for his product design, it does not necessarily mean the product is manufactured and tested to this design. The following are a couple of real-life examples.

Formerly, as the manufacturing manager for a company that was not yet compliant with a product safety standard (and law in some cities) called "LULU," I went to the sales organization for guidance to identify the first product to be brought into compliance to minimize any potential losses. The head salesperson gave me some guidance but assured me that this new law would not affect the company's sales performance or his incentive plan. When I inquired how that was possible, he winked and opened his drawer. Out came a roll of LULU stickers he was placing on the products in the distribution center.

In another job as a new director of manufacturing, I decided to spend my second day on the assembly lines meeting the employees and going through the assembly process. This product spent most of its life in dark and damp locations and would accommodate 220 volts. It also carried a Canadian safety sticker. When I got to the end of the assembly line, I noticed that there was no earth-to-ground dielectric test being performed. This test ensures that customers are safe from shock. When I inquired why this test was not performed, I was told it was a pain to perform and it slowed things down, so my predecessor had removed it. I then asked how they were able to slip this by the visiting Canadian inspector, upon which I was told that when he showed up, they told him they weren't building anything for Canada then, and he went away.

If your buyers have a choice between buying from a certified or a noncertified supplier, and they choose the possibly cheaper, noncertified supplier's product, they may face a much grimmer liability situation.

Certified Organizations Focused On Continuous Improvement

In the 1990s, organizational success will be determined by a few key factors. One of these is speed. Execution speed includes the speed of product development, product upgrade and introduction, and even the more mundane functions such as responding to a customer inquiry. Speed will determine who are the profitable leaders and who are the less fortunate followers.

Speed comes from the repetition of well-defined tasks coupled with the continuous improvement of the supporting operating systems. If a competitor is able to perfect a working quality model before you do, they will begin to pick up competitive speed, and with speed comes distance. The longer you wait, the greater the distance you fall behind your competitors.

While their speed picks up, your organization, without the working model, will begin to slow down as you divert resources to brute-forcing results, all the while your resources become further diminished due to decreasing sales. Soon you are caught in a vicious cycle with the only possible solutions being painful ones — if it's not too late altogether.

Here's an outline of such a decline. Your sales organization probably has a tough job winning business in a normal environment, where all competitors are on par. If your organization is having difficulties with product quality, response time, or delivery integrity, the first part of your salesperson's call time is usually spent apologizing and sorting the performance problems before being able to do his sales pitch on the benefits of your products. You are losing a lot of selling time and reducing the effectiveness of sales presentation time. And that's on top of the customer's displeasure with your late delivery, which violates the number one quality priority and for which this customer is now personally taking the heat from his management.

If the problem is persistent, your sales people may never get the chance to sell at all, or worse yet, not meet their sales incentive plan. You can burn through good sales people quickly and they will become excellent competitors who know all your weaknesses. It doesn't take long to lose a customer, but it takes quite a bit longer and requires more resources to get those customers back than if you had stabilized your business.

Media Awareness

Achieving ISO 9000 registration is a newsworthy event — take full advantage of it. Consider the news of your certification just as you would any major event in your company, such as a major new product introduction or the appointment of a new senior executive. Get your marketing and communications specialists onboard early (plan on six months before certification), educate them, and let them educate the media in your industry and formulate the strategy to maximize the visibility of this landmark achievement. If you're thinking of the costs associated with advertising, think again. Save the money to fly your quality guru around to all of your customers to help them get certified. Remember, the healthier your customers are, the healthier you will be. Effective public relations will get you much better visibility at only a fraction of the cost. Next, think about further merchandising your achievement by placing your registration mark on your literature, business cards, invoices, and company letterhead. Do not put the registration mark on your product. Certification is a "good housekeeping" seal for your business and in no way infers product fitness (in fact, you can lose your certification for such an offense). In addition, don't forget to train your sales force on what ISO 9000 is and prepare them to answer questions and show the certificate. Did you ever hear of a CEO that didn't want to hear about how to make significant improvements in corporate performance? When used properly, ISO 9000 could make the difference between your sales force gaining access to the executive suite over your competition.

Customer Perception

Tom Peters, in his book, *Thriving on Chaos*, describes the results of the PIMS (Profit Impact of Market Strategy) study, conducted by the Strategic Planning Institute (Cambridge, MA). This study found that high market share provides profits, however, long-term market share comes from "perceived product or service quality." Perceived means as seen through the customers' eyes rather than the producers'. The study also found that changes in quality have a significantly greater effect on market share than price.

In James Sewel's book, *Customers For Life*, the author illustrates how effective the concept of perceived quality can be when coupled with a structured system for customer satisfaction. He presents the results of a study in which his Cadillac dealership with a focus on service and customer perception is compared with Cadillac dealers nationwide, demonstrating how two identical cars can be perceived completely differently. The following table illustrates the percentage of customers who indicated they would purchase the same make:

	Sewel's	Nationwide
Definitely	47%	35%
Probably Not	9%	13%
Definitely Not	3%	9%

It can cost up to five times more to win a new customer than it does to keep an existing one. Sewel's example demonstrates a remarkable advantage over the other Cadillac dealers as well as other manufacturers of similar vehicles. A Gallup poll asked what people were willing to pay for a product that they perceived as having higher than average quality. The results were:

• Approximately 30% more for a better car.
• Approximately 50% more for a better household appliance.
• Approximately 200% more for a better low-price personal item.

Sewel's results, combined with the Gallup poll, clearly demonstrate the business need to generate high levels of perceived quality for your company and its products. ISO 9000 certification offers a clear, readily understandable criterion for evaluation.

ISO 9000 has become the base quality standard for the U.S. The American National Standards Institute (ANSI) has adopted and renamed it as the ANSI/ASQC Q9000-1 series. As certification to the standard becomes more common, your customers will use it as a means of evaluation. If you can demonstrate certification, you will save your customer the cost of evaluation and it will also reduce your costs as customer audits go down. You can spend more time with your customers developing products or helping them figure out how you can both reduce your cycle times and total costs.

When will this happen? Will it become a U.S. requirement as well as a European one? There is no easy answer, but we believe it will be soon. If the experience in the U.K. is any indicator, it took about a year for the awareness to grow and for certification to begin for the BS 5750 code. Before it became an EC adopted standard, growth was consistent at about 50% per year, as seen in Figure 3.4. Registration of U.S. operations to ISO 9000 is growing dramatically as seen in Figure 3.5. According to Mark Morrow, editor of *Quality Systems Update*, a newsletter dedicated to the issues associated with ISO 9000 (Figure 3.6), hundreds of companies are now on the threshold of receiving certification and the number of certified U.S. owned facilities is growing geometrically, very similar to the U.K. A listing of certified facilities in the U.S. and Canada has been compiled by *Quality Systems Update,* as shown in Figure 3.7.

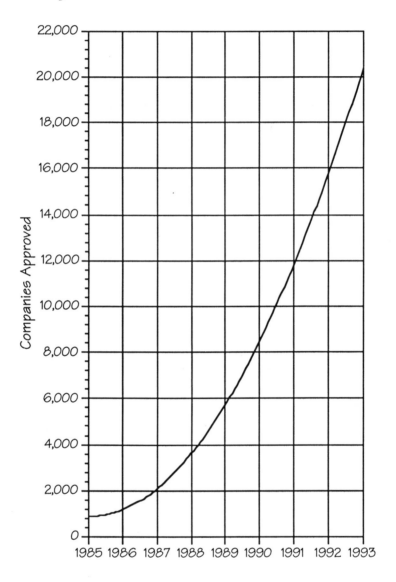

Figure 3.4 *Growth in U.K. third-party certification of quality management systems. Source: Det Norske Veritas.*

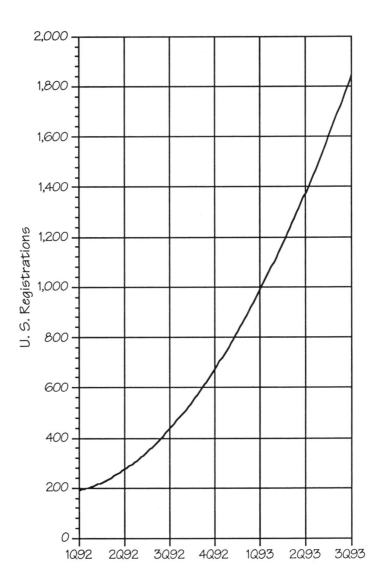

Figure 3.5 Growth in ISO 9000 registrations in the U.S.
Source: Quality Systems Update

A Global ISO 9000 Forum And Information Service

Volume 3, Number 1   January 1993

Number of Registered Sites Grows Exponentially
Sites In Nearly 50 States

Acceptance of the ISO 9000 series standards continues to explode across the United States and Canada with a total of 621 registered companies in the U.S. and 278 in Canada.

Unofficial records maintained by *QSU* also show that registered companies are located in 45 of the 50 states. The only states without a single registered company are Alaska, Hawaii, Idaho, Montana and Wyoming, plus the District of Columbia.

The U.S. total, as of December 21, represents an increase of 221 companies since a similar survey in July, and an increase of 396 companies since one in February. The Canadian figure represents an increase of 77 companies since July.

Differing Registration Approaches

The statistics highlight a significant distinction between Canadian and U.S. companies. Most U.S. firms have pursued registration to the ISO 9001-9002 external quality assurance standards while Canadian firms have overwhelmingly sought registration under ISO 9003, the least comprehensive standard in the series.

Unlike the other two external standards, ISO 9003 addresses only the requirements for detection and control of problems during final inspection and testing. It applies to organizations whose products or services can be adequately assessed by testing and inspection. This gener-

ally refers to less-complex products or services.

A total of 220 U.S. firms are registered under ISO 9001, 374 under ISO 9002 and 21 under ISO 9003. By comparison, only 29 Canadian firms are registered under ISO 9001 and 62 under ISO 9002. The remaining 187 are registered under ISO 9003. In past surveys, this difference has been attributed to the fact that many of the Canadian sites are merely distribution centers for products manufactured elsewhere.

Lone Star Leader

Texas, with 75 registered companies, continues to lead the nation *(see NUMBERS, page 8)*

Misleading Advertising Concerns Standards Bodies

A series of ads running in computer magazines that depict the doddering cartoon character Mr. Magoo heralding a so-called "ISO 9001 Award of Reliability" has been criticized by officials of the International Organization for Standardization (ISO).

The ads contain a number of false claims and represent one of the "worst" examples of misleading advertising based on company registration to the ISO 9000 series standards, according to Jacques Blanc, Geneva-based ISO's director of application and information.

Standards bodies and registrars are increasingly wary of advertising

claims made by companies anxious to broadcast their registration to ISO 9000-series standards. The problem could grow in the U.S. as more companies become registered and use their status as a marketing tool.

The Magoo ad is for Samtron Displays Inc., which manufactures computer monitors. Samtron is a subsidiary of Korea-based Samsung Electron Devices Co. Ltd.

The ad, which appeared in the Nov. 16 issue of *Info World* and other magazines, has a drawing of Magoo perched atop a dog. The character is holding up an ISO 9001 sign:

"Now even reliability is easy to *(see ADVERTISING, page 15)*

Figure 3.6 As the events and issues associated with ISO 9000 unravel, Quality Systems Update keeps you up-to-date with the latest developments.

ISO 9000

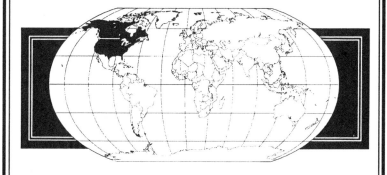

REGISTERED COMPANY DIRECTORY

United States & Canada

Summer 1992 Update

compiled by

Quality Systems Update

An International Forum & Information Service

Figure 3.7 This directory of certified companies within the U.S. and Canada, published and updated by Quality Systems Update, will allow a purchasing agent to quickly determine whether your company or manufacturing site has been certified to the ISO 9000 standard.

Internal Organizational Health

Remember, ISO 9000 ensures that a foundation for good business practice is in place. It also forces a linkage between organizations and improves communications. ISO 9000 will cause a gradual improvement in your operation as it requires implementation of a corrective action process. However, it adds a major competitive advantage in its support of your overall quality improvement program, that is, the profitable growth part. This foundation will allow you to meet the challenge of true quality:

Quality is exceeding your customer's expectations while maintaining profitable growth.

This quality definition can be further broken down to the "seven P's." You need all seven to consistently exceed your customer's expectations and the P's are supported by ISO 9000 as well.

1. Product performance to customers' specification.
2. Perception by customers that needs are exceeded in all areas.
3. Progressive improvement of performance
   (to meet growing customer expectations).
4. Process stability as a foundation for speed and accuracy.
5. Profitability that allows further investment and growth.
6. People empowerment
   (the driving force for meeting customer expectations).
7. Partnership (customers and suppliers).

ISO 9000 has far-reaching implications beyond procedures and documentation. Conformance will not only get you onto the global playing field, but it will also effect positive organizational change, improve your competitive position, enhance your company's market perception, and ultimately improve your bottom line. The choice is yours.

4

The Road To Discovery

For most companies, ISO 9000 will either augment ongoing quality efforts or spark a renewed emphasis on quality. This chapter will describe the events surrounding the certification process of The Foxboro Company, an 85-year-old New England manufacturer of measurement instruments and systems for process automation, to ISO 9001. Like many manufacturers today, the Foxboro Company had to adjust its paradigms for business in the 1990s. ISO 9000 played a major role in achieving this adjustment.

Among the First to Achieve ISO 9000 Certification

The Foxboro Company develops, manufactures, engineers, and integrates control systems, analytical instruments, and sensing and control devices for the process industries. Its products measure and automate processes in industries such as pulp and paper, oil refining, utilities, pharmaceuticals, food products, mining, and steel production. Foxboro was a Fortune 500 company through September 1990, when it was purchased by Siebe plc, a U.K.-based engineering and controls company traded on the London Stock Exchange.

The Foxboro Company was one of the first companies in the United States to become fully certified to ISO 9001. A short time later, its joint-venture manufacturing plant in the People's Republic of China became certified to ISO 9001, making it the first company to achieve any form of ISO 9000 certification in the P.R.C. While Foxboro has aggressively pursued ISO 9000, the real story is the role ISO played in the turnaround of the company's quality efforts. The following story is a tribute to the employees of The Foxboro Company — their collective efforts were instrumental in achieving ISO 9001 registration.

Evolution to ISO 9000

At Foxboro, we are first to admit that we don't have all the answers, nor do we believe we will ever get to that point. After more than four years into our TQM journey, we realize that we have just begun.

We learned from our initial World Class Manufacturing (WCM) lessons that process stability is critical for success, and we applied this knowledge across the entire enterprise. What started out as a WCM effort has grown to become a World Class Enterprise (WCE) effort with ongoing positive results.

A few years ago, a cartoon by Gary Larson of *The Far Side* described Foxboro's situation in the mid-1980s. It pictured a dinosaur behind a podium addressing a conference of dinosaurs, with the caption, "The picture's pretty bleak, gentlemen... the world's climates are changing, the mammals are taking over, and we all have a brain about the size of a walnut." We were experiencing dramatic change. Unless we began to focus and use our intelligence, we would have suffered the same fate.

In the 1960s and 1970s, Foxboro was the dominant player in the process control industry; our margins were good, and the world was our oyster — as it seemed for many companies. In the midst of our success, we became complacent and failed to notice that the climate was rapidly changing. We suddenly encountered new domestic and foreign competitors who were aggressive and hungry. We watched our business environment deteriorate, and, for quite a while, we just tried to wish it away. Our first major restructuring occurred in 1985 followed by another in 1987. Even after we began our Total Quality journey at Foxboro, we continued to pay the price for our earlier lack of responsiveness. If employee population is a measure of pain, ours was significant. Our employment plummeted from a high of 12,000 in 1985 to its current level of 4,000. Yet today we ship roughly three times more per employee than we did in 1985. Although it was sad to see the departure of so many people, the future for those remaining is very bright.

In 1987, the Touche Ross consulting group asked the Foxboro Company to participate in an industry-wide study to identify the factors critical for a company to achieve World-Class status. The group benchmarked various automation suppliers to determine the critical factors for success. The results made it clear that Foxboro would need to embrace the following principles if we were to survive:

> "There will be no safe harbor from the onslaught of competition" — we were already witnessing the wave. No industry is secure, however, as is shown by the crippled giants of the past.

> "Thresholds for performance will continually increase." The strong capabilities of today will become the mediocre performances of tomorrow. Process capabilities must improve, and speed will determine the winners.

> "The leaders in the market will dictate the standards." If we seize the lead, we can set the standards that would cause our competitors to follow. If you aren't the leader, your profits will reflect your "me too" status.

> "To remain viable you must always attempt to exceed the new standards" — realizing that it takes time to get there, and by the time you do achieve your goal, the standard probably will have grown to meet your improvement.

> "Quality will be the number one requirement for customer satisfaction in the 1990s."

> "Quality is to be defined by our customers, regardless of what we believed." Our customers will point the way. Those companies that are able to maintain a close relationship with their customers will gain the greatest

understanding of their requirements, and in turn, will
have the opportunity to produce the best product for the
customer first. Those companies that are able to demonstrate conformance to their customers' standards will
enjoy market share.

We now believe that ISO 9000 certification is a conformance standard that our friends at Touche Ross were foretelling. We use these
guidelines and are aggressively communicating our position and commitment to this quality issue to our customers. Being one of the first
companies to meet this hurdle demonstrates our commitment to them.
Quality has become one of our weapons, and we are determined to
continue to improve.

The competitive benchmarking efforts reinforced the need to improve our competitive position. As we were conducting our survey with
Touche Ross, our customers were also beginning to give us signals that
indeed the climate had changed and we were looking at extinction if we
did not migrate toward quality. The following is just one example.

TQM Recognized

As mentioned in a previous chapter, in 1979, the Ford Motor Company
recalled more cars than it produced. At that time, Dr. Deming advised
Ford of the need for process integrity and the need to get its suppliers
involved. He pointed out that unless it could control its processes, all of
its other efforts would be in vain. When Ford's customers sat inside a
Ford vehicle they actually saw Ford's suppliers, in this case, the suppliers
of upholstery and carpeting. Deming said that these suppliers had to
deliver a quality product and continually improve their product simultaneously with Ford. The supplier as well as Ford needed to have an
active quality program.

The only way a company could ensure a high-quality product was to
select high-quality suppliers of materials and tools—this meant a supplier that not only produced a high-quality product, but did so consistently. Suppliers who met this objective would enjoy Ford's business.

Ford took the initiative with its "Quality is Job #1" program. Ten years later, Ford is still advertising it. Ford also took Dr. Deming's advice and went to its suppliers; in this case, the supplier of fabrics was told to put together a quality program that would deliver a quality product coming from a quality process focused on continuous improvement. That supplier later went on to win the Baldrige Award.

As shown in Figure 4.1, Ford told the supplier it wanted consistent color and a fabric that would last for the life of the car. The fabric supplier also recognized that raw material consistency was the key to its success. It could not produce consistent color or keep the threads from breaking without robust and consistent raw materials. The supplier, in turn, went to its raw material supplier and restated Ford's requirements. The raw material supplier certainly did not want to lose one of its customers, so it cooperated and set up a quality program as well. As it was establishing a quality program, it quickly discovered the lessons learned at Ford and began to work with its own suppliers.

Enter Foxboro, the supplier that provided the equipment that controlled the process used to manufacture the raw materials. The message was the same all the way down the supplier chain. "Get your process under control, focus on continuous improvement, implement a Total Quality Management program, or get out!" At that point in time, however, things were not all well at Foxboro:

• New product development was not keeping ahead of the competition.
• Waste and yields were not being aggressively pursued.
• We launched a "bet the company" product prematurely.
• Deliveries across all product lines were unreliable.
• Our customer satisfaction was at an all-time low.

In late 1987, one of Foxboro's vice-presidents was called down to the raw material manufacturer and told to either get a quality program or look for a new customer. Adding this to what we had heard earlier from Touche Ross, Foxboro responded in a classic, knee-jerk fashion, "let's go out quickly and buy a program." On a Friday, we bought a quality

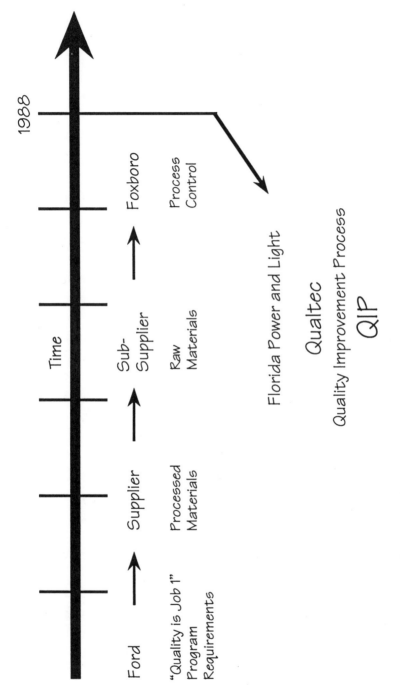

Figure 4.1 Origins of TQM at The Foxboro Company.

module from one quality consultant, and by the following Tuesday, we purchased an entirely different program from another quality practitioner. But we got lucky. The program we finally settled on, QIP (Quality Improvement Process) from Qualtec Quality Services, Inc. (a Florida Power and Light company), has satisfied our needs and served us well (see Figure 4.2).

QIP met our cultural and financial needs, it was supported by Qualtec (an outside agency that could provide constancy), it was modular and structured for easy deployment in our organization, and most important, our senior management was behind it, thereby, providing the management constancy needed to make it succeed. QIP has become one key ingredient in Foxboro's TQM program.

The practice of this quality improvement process contributed to Florida Power and Light's winning of the prestigious Japanese Deming Award. With a purchased program and a consultant in hand, we embarked on our quest for quality improvement.

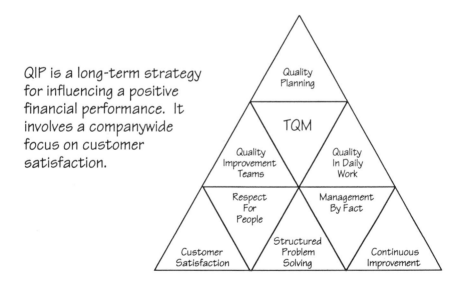

QIP is a long-term strategy for influencing a positive financial performance. It involves a companywide focus on customer satisfaction.

Figure 4.2 QIP at Foxboro based on Qualtec's program.

QIP at Foxboro

Foxboro's QIP program, introduced in 1989, consists of five strategic elements.

1 • Customer Satisfaction – Take care of your customer. Determine their concerns, make sure you can fix them, and begin working on it.

2 • Management by Fact – The only way to run a business; gut feelings don't count.

3 • Structured Problem Solving – Use a structured problem-solving process that focuses on the root cause of a problem, and then methodically implement upgrades that affect the root cause. "Band-Aid" approaches don't work — this process fixes long-term problems that have eluded quick fixes.

4 • Respect for People – It is no longer the person who postures and pounds fists that gets the respect. It's the individual who can build consensus within a group and empower employees to go out and satisfy customers. It's also those people who can cause constancy in an organization and make the group move quickly.

5 • Continuous Improvement – This is a mind-set that Henry Ford perfected and talked about in his book *Today and Tomorrow,* written in 1926. Once your employees realize that all jobs can be improved, it becomes a way of life and the defenses come down.

Foxboro employees are trained in these elements through their participation in QIP teams. Each team consists of five to seven employees who receive a week of training. In addition, each team has a Team Leader who is trained for an additional week and a Facilitator who is trained for three weeks. The team uses a structured problem-solving process, utilizing the statistical and analytical tools they have been trained on, and follows a storyboard approach, as seen in Figure 4.3.

The team focuses on a common customer and goes about addressing the "tall pole" problems — those few problems that cause the majority of the pain — that this customer is experiencing. The good news is that the teams solve long-term problems. The better news is that the team members take the training they have received back to their regular jobs.

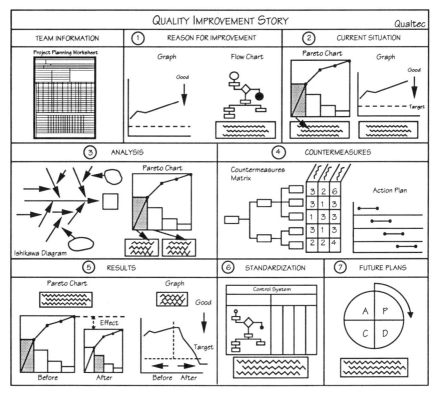

Figure 4.3 Storyboard used with the QIP problem-solving process.

We have seen a steady growth in the number of teams and their benefit to the company. For example, when attending a meeting, it is rare not to see a PAL (Purpose, Agenda & Limit) and enforcement of the QIP meeting rules of conduct. We are seeing a cultural change with more than 1,000 employees trained in the QIP process.

The QIP program and teams began in early 1989 with excellent growth and results; over 120 active teams currently participate. The contribution of the first 13 teams returned more than $1 million in very real savings while generating unmeasurable positive returns in customer satisfaction. QIP teams, however, are not a "do everything" tool. The QIP team storyboard approach solves long-term problems systematically, in a structured environment. The solutions are very effective, but it does not happen quickly, nor does it cause radical or rapid change. In addition, it is not the only method to achieve customer satisfaction. In fact, Mr. Crosby, the quality guru, warns of a single-solution approach; beware of the "Happy Meals" syndrome, where everything comes in a neat box.

In mid-1989, Foxboro's new Vice President of Manufacturing (and later President) realized that we had to break out of our prior manufacturing paradigm, and quickly. To this end, he initiated the World Class Manufacturing Program which has since grown into Foxboro's TQM program, as seen in Figure 4.4.

World Class Manufacturing (WCM)

Foxboro's program included many of the concepts found in Richard J. Schonberger's book, *World Class Manufacturing,* while recognizing that most of these concepts were not new and, in fact, can be traced back to Henry Ford. The program also adopted the beliefs of leaders like Deming, Juran, Crosby, Feigenbaum, and a host of contemporary Japanese experts.

For Foxboro, WCM was an empowerment program. If as an employee you were focused on any of the key components of the program and you were communicating with your fellow employees to assure everyone was coordinated, you were encouraged to pursue it.

External Customer Requirements

Being world class meant that we had to reexamine who our customers were. As it turned out they were not only the "end users," but also the sales people, customer engineering, and our distributors. Of course, manufacturing wasn't talking to any of them on a regular basis. Therefore, we sat down with each of these groups and asked what was important to them from a process perspective. The following paragraphs illustrate what they told us.

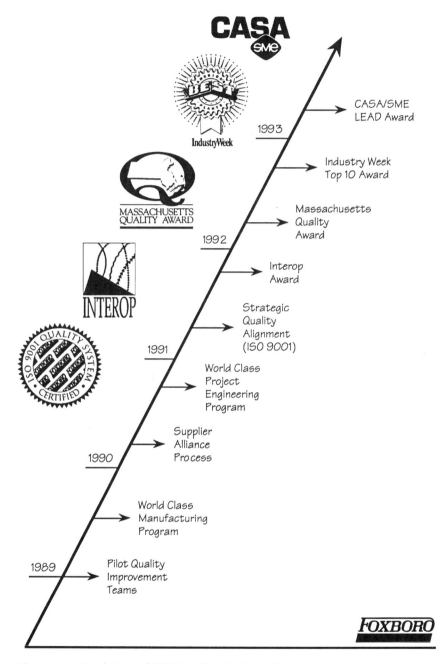

Figure 4.4 Evolution of TQM at The Foxboro Company.

Product – Reduce your variability; the product specification is just a minimum. One of the larger customers showed us the importance of product variability and how it impacts their operations. Delivering a product to specification was no longer good enough. We had to reduce the variability.

Delivery integrity – This was the most important measure of quality as expressed by our customers' buyers. The buyers are driven by two major factors. Did the product arrive on time? What is my purchase price variance? We realized we could never get beyond the buyers to sell our products if we did not perform on that first measure.

Process – They understand that if our processes exhibit a high level of process integrity (control), they are far more likely to receive a good product, on time, at the lowest total cost to them. In fact, our customers pointed out that we could not consistently deliver any of their requirements unless we had our processes under control. Here's the example they used. "Foxboro could send a salesperson in at $200 per call in expenses 50 times during a three-year period. It takes just one site inspection on our part to determine that your processes are not under control, making your $10,000 investment worthless. So, Foxboro, put your money into process integrity, then call on us."

Reduce your lead times – "In most cases, stay competitive but figure out a way we can obtain small quantities quickly. In some cases, we receive last minute changes to our order and need the response." This is critical to our distributors, because even though they stock products, they undergo surges and wanes. The more we make them wait, the more they have to stock, which incurs cost. This cost is borne by the end users, or worse, enjoyed by the competition.

Increase your flexibility – This is the improved ability to call out various configurations in modular combinations. They also spoke of flexibility in terms of delivery crisis. One of our customers had experienced a serious freeze that damaged their plant. They needed 250 instruments to get up and running, and of course this happened over the Christmas shutdown. In response to a desperate customer, Foxboro called in a large work force and had the instruments in the air within two days. No operation outside Foxboro could stock for that type of demand, and our customers depend on that capability.

Administration – A QIP team with a customer taught us something we had never really given much thought to. Even though our instrument price was less than our competitors, when the customer received the instrument and couldn't match it with the order paperwork, the customer spent $130 trying to reconcile the two, making our instrument more expensive. But, we were also told that if we could put the customer's inventory location and instructions on the upper right hand corner of the box, we could reduce the cost by $30, making our instrument much less expensive than our competitors'. This customer was looking at the *total cost* of doing business and realized that the purchase price was usually a small fraction of the Total Cost of Ownership. We also need to mention that not allowing our customers to easily match our invoices with material received frustrates their receiving operations, which is usually tied into the materials organizations (where the buyers are located). When they can't receive your material easily, they have a tendency not to pay you very quickly, which then puts pressure on your receivables department. They, in turn, further harass your customer for prompt payment and your relationship with your customer deteriorates.

New and improved products that support the lowest life-cycle cost – If we can invest in a product component that extends the mean-time-between-failure from 15 years to 30, we will do it. If we can produce a device that requires calibration only once a year versus twice, we will go ahead with the improvement, even if it does cost significantly more, because then our customer would have to bear the cost of sending out a crew to calibrate the instrument or replace it or possibly shut down an operation generating revenue at a rate of thousands of dollars per minute. Our customers are becoming very astute on the issue of total cost. The purchase price of a product is just a fraction of the total cost of a product.

Concurrent development – Our customers have unique competitive opportunities with limited windows to capture market share or where small savings can account for large earnings. A good supplier will quickly move with its customers to help them capture the opportunity and will develop a structured ongoing relationship that will support customers' needs. At Foxboro, that means not only a formal relationship with our customers, but a formal program to integrate our suppliers in the rapid development and delivery of new and competitive products. Simply, our customers were asking us to help them become more competitive — that's what it's all about. You won't be successful if your people don't know their roles and the system remains undefined. ISO 9000 compliance addresses the success of your organization because it addresses these two factors. Supporting these defined customer needs required us to restructure the way we planned and carried out our business. We looked to the visionaries and incorporated their messages.

Strategic Components

Foxboro put in place a series of strategic manufacturing endeavors that incorporated the concepts of Deming and Juran, as seen in Figure 4.5. One involved a cultural change toward quality by driving Management Constancy through the use of various councils focused on the weak areas cited by our customers.

We also developed a series of performance measures that focused on continual improvement of the process used to satisfy our customers and carried out programs that ensured that our employees were heard and became involved. This included training in structured problem solving, quality tools, and JIT/TQC methods that focused on the elimination of waste and promotion of customer satisfaction.

We began a series of process upgrades to simplify how business was conducted. Finally, we completed the model with a series of cost reduction activities again focused on the reduction of nonvalue-added activities and redundancies.

As these programs were progressing, we began to encounter organizational roadblocks. They weren't over the destination but rather the methods and the standards to be used to reach the destination. The individuals involved, all excellent in their respective fields, brought along

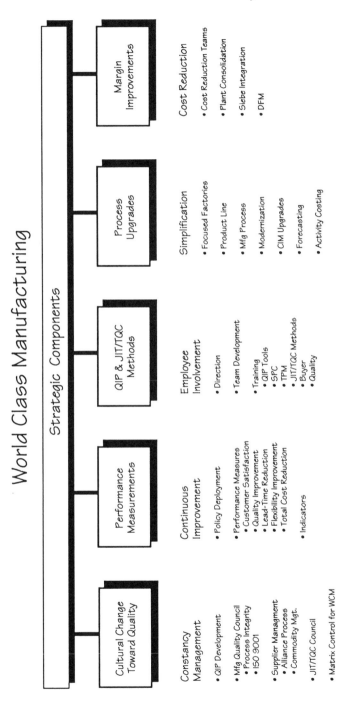

Figure 4.5 Strategic components of Foxboro's World Class Manufacturing program.

differing perspectives and experience. Fortunately, they all adhered to the one universal truth of managing a business — Customer Satisfaction.

It is not that any of these people aren't excellent in their professions; it's just that their environment, training, and past are different. Customer satisfaction is the only universal truth when it comes to managing a business.

This truth got us back on track. Again our customers pointed us in the right direction, to the ISO 9000 standard. At about the same time, our own senior quality people began telling us about the standard and suggested this might be a solution.

We looked at ISO 9000 and discovered that it addressed our entire business. It defined standards and expectations while accommodating a wide range of organizations and their uniqueness.

The manufacturing quality council adopted the standard and began integrating it into the manufacturing operations. We soon saw it had far wider implications than just manufacturing improvement.

Supplier Alliance Program

The Supplier Alliance program was initiated to capture the benefits derived from a group of excellent suppliers integrated into our organization.

Foxboro over the years had adopted the mind-set that somehow we had to build everything and had established an infrastructure and overhead to match that expectation. We were not inclined to integrate our suppliers and capture the speed and excellence they were capable of offering. While business was growing rapidly and competitive pressures were low, this strategy masked a poor manufacturing policy. Once competition intensified, however, the overhead and inefficiencies prevented us from moving quickly.

As we began the supplier integration, we recognized that it was necessary not only to change how we selected our suppliers, but also to change how we managed our side of the business. We have broken down the traditional supplier/buyer organization and migrated to a commodity team management style. Our suppliers are now managed according to a philosophy that requires that both parties win, and they are involved in mutual continuous improvement and waste-elimination activities. We have seen some spectacular returns in waste reduction, improvements in lead times and flexibility, and new product introductions.

We also believe that by assisting our suppliers with their efforts, we will both enjoy their success. As of this writing, we have trained more than 550 suppliers during four large ISO 9000 training sessions.

World Class Project Engineering

One of the direct benefits to come from our ISO 9000 preparation was the discovery of our "Work Breakdown Structure" (WBS) methodology for doing business within our project engineering operations. This is an example of how the ISO 9000 team sought the best way to conduct business and meet the requirements of the standard. We have four industry engineering groups, each of which ran its operations in a unique fashion. As the team went through the ISO 9000 preparation process, they discovered that one of the groups had a much better defined process and its customers seemed to be responding more favorably. The projects came in on time and the group seemed to have their projects under better control and yielding a consistently higher margin. This became the standard for all our industry engineering operations. Now all our engineering groups are using the standard, people are interchangeable, and we are now even using the same symbols. The result is on-time projects, happy customers, cost control, reusable engineering, and savings of more than $1 million per year by reducing waste.

The WBS, as seen in Figure 4.6, breaks down a customer's needs into distinct phases and identifies the tasks, responsibilities, resource needs, and costs within each phase, enabling you to deliver a project within budget and on time. This gives you a competitive advantage, as long as you communicate your ability to the customer.

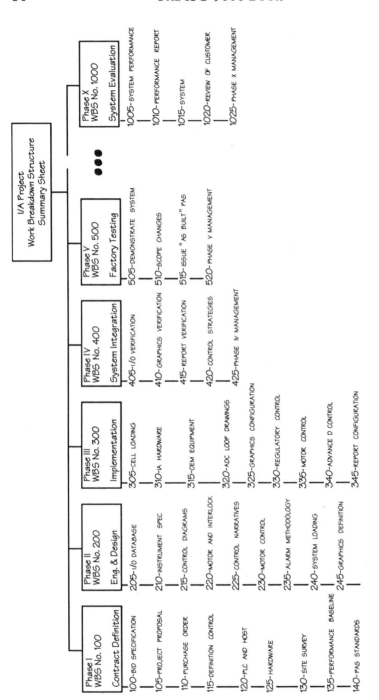

Figure 4.6 Work Breakdown Structure methodology used for world-class project execution.

Strategic Quality Alignment — Going for ISO 9001

Many positive programs were underway in the company. Real progress and positive results were being realized. But something was still missing. A common framework for running the business was needed that would not only provide a communications structure (procedures), but a means for transcending organizational boundaries to derive greater synergy among operations — in other words, a vehicle for creating a Strategic Quality Alignment of all our ongoing activities. The more we looked at and became aware of ISO 9000, we realized that it would provide the solution. We recognized that we needed to move ahead quickly for our own organizational health as well as to address the competitive issues described in the previous chapter.

We recognized that ISO 9000 would become a global standard and a basic minimum hurdle for doing business. We also expected to gain a competitive advantage by being one of the first to become certified. It would provide a visible example that Foxboro's quality approach was aggressive and committed to a Total Quality endeavor. As it turns out, it has also given us the opportunity to share our ISO 9001 certification experience with our customers. We regularly hold orientation and training sessions with them. It's cementing our relationship and in some cases putting our competitors in a defensive position.

The final and, in fact, the primary reason we began this journey was that of organizational health. We just knew it would make us a better company.

In March of 1991, we achieved what we term "Strategic Quality Alignment." This is significant not only because we became a fully certified company with the successful certification of all our domestic manufacturing operations (see Figure 4.7), but it was at that point that we had evolved our efforts into a working quality model. ISO 9001 certification was merely a milestone marker in our TQM journey.

A short time later, our joint-venture manufacturing plant in the People's Republic of China became certified to ISO 9001, making it the first company to achieve any form of ISO 9000 certification in the P.R.C. (see Figure 4.8).

Figure 4.7 The Foxboro Company was one of the first major U.S. companies to achieve ISO 9001 certification.

Certificate No. QSC 3043

DET NORSKE
VERITAS

质 量 体 系 合 格 证

经审核,中国 上海 漕宝路 161 号
上海·福克斯波罗有限公司
的质量体系符合质量体系标准:

ISO 9001

特发此证。
本合格证对下列的生产/服务范围有效:
变送器及电子测量和控制系统的销售、工程技术、系统设计 造和技术服务。

质量体系文件编号:	ROT 91.3020	日期: 1991 年 11 月 20 日
审计报告编号:	ROT 91.3021	日期: 1991 年 12 月 20 日
合格证有效期:	1991 年 12 月 20 日 至 1994 年 12 月 20 日	

根据 1991 年 12 月 20 日签署的定期审计办法(编号 NO.QSC3043)规定,如果未能通过
定期 的审计,本合格证将失效。

Det norske Veritas   日期: 1991 年 12 月 20 日

经 理 代 表   主 审 计 师
G.B. 卡斯特伯格   A. 特 威 勒

G.B. Casberg   A. ter Weele

Figure 4.8 The Shanghai-Foxboro Company was the first company to achieve any form of ISO 9000 certification in the People's Republic of China.

TQM: A Working Model

With our model in place, as shown in Figure 4.9, we have:
- A company being trained in five basic principles and tools via Qualtec's QIP team approach (changing the culture).
- Continuous improvement driven by quality teams. We support more than 120 QIP teams and a greater number of less formal "Process Excellence Teams" (PETs) composed of groups such as World Class Manufacturing teams, Costs Reduction teams, JIT/TQC teams, DPU/ 2 teams, etc.
- We now have a tool, ISO 9000, that ensures a structured working environment that captures improvements and integrates them into a stable and structured operation, thereby keeping those good ideas from eroding.
- Finally, we have a management structure that actively supports and nurtures the model. It plans and executes around a matrixed decision

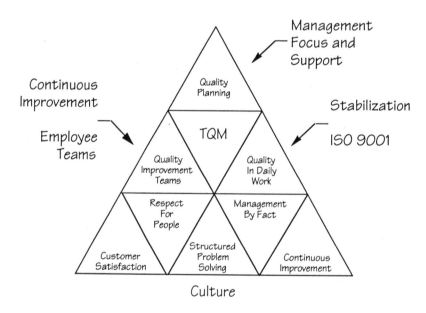

Figure 4.9 TQM: A working model.

and execution process. It promotes a working environment that respects and supports the employees who deliver Customer Satisfaction and Quality.

With a working model in place, we are able to support the structure with a series of drivers that translate the model into working vehicles. These drivers add guidance to the vehicles that carry the program into a series of actions creating the TQM climate focused on Customer Satisfaction and Quality.

At the end of the day, the real questions that must be asked are, what has all this done for our customers? How have we helped our customers?

TQM and ISO 9000 Benefits

As noted earlier, our customers asked for *delivery integrity* and *process stability*. They said they wanted us to *reduce waste* and the *total cost* of doing business with Foxboro. They needed a *quality product* that focused on their needs and that of their customers. The following are just some of the results we've realized as we move down the TQM path.

Delivery integrity – We are now in Baldrige winner country, but we aren't getting too carried away with our greater than 98% on-time figure (see Figure 4.10). We ship approximately 40,000 instruments and pieces of equipment every month. At 98% on-time we are still making 800 customers unhappy per month. While we have made progress, we still have a long way to go.

Plant inventories – In terms of waste reduction, we were able to cut our inventories in half. Henry Ford spends a lot of time in his book talking about inventory as waste. As we improved our processes, the inventory required was reduced, as seen in Figure 4.11. This was the equivalent of increasing sales by $60 million! Remarkably, at the same time, we improved delivery performance by 20%. Historically, inventory was perceived as an insurance policy against delivery shortfall.

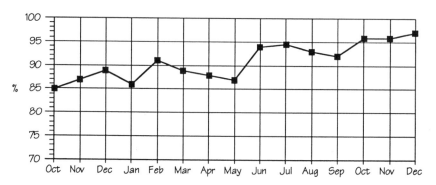

4.10 Delivery Integrity (% On Time). Delivery integrity for all Foxboro products has improved significantly since the introduction of TQM.

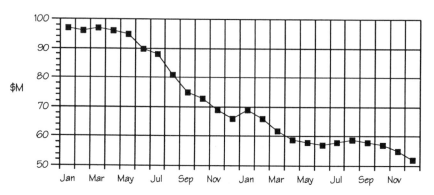

4.11 Inventory ($M). Total inventories have been reduced dramatically, contributing to waste elimination and cost reductions.

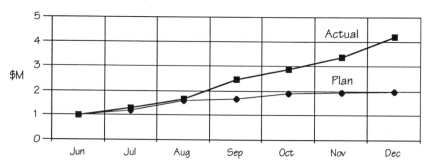

4.12 Product Cost Reductions ($M). TQM has played a major role in product cost reductions.

Material cost reductions – Total cost reduction takes many forms. In our systems manufacturing operations, we were able to trim our material cost by more than $4 million (see Figure 4.12). This was achieved by teams of employees getting together and looking at our products and seeing where they could make them better while reducing the costs. The ground rules are simple; cost reduction can only occur when the products' mean time between failure has been maintained or improved. We saved more than 5% in material costs across the company using this team-focused approach.

Employee involvement – We asked our employees in those areas where they traditionally were not subject to rigorous procedures and structure requirements what they thought of this effort. Their feedback is summarized below and listed in Figure 4.13:

We have consistency, not dependent on any one individual. – As you remove the redundancy from your organization and trim down, it becomes exceedingly important that people can step in for others, that they have been trained such that the operation doesn't come to a complete stop. It is also critical that the functions are all done in the same fashion and thus reduce variation. This occurred with one of our quality teams as we were installing our ISO 9000 program. This team was attempting to reduce defects occurring over a three-shift operation of a group that was only achieving a mid-60% yield on their finished product. The team looked at the problem and discovered that each operator on each shift performed the job differently. Each tweaked the equipment to what they thought produced the best product. As the materials moved through this operation, there were tremendous tolerance "stack-ups" resulting in a tremendous waste of materials. By having all three shifts develop and agree on a single machining and assembly methodology, the yields are now higher than 95%.

There is a home for good ideas. – This might be one of the most powerful aspects of ISO 9000, as employees only contribute when they know they will be heard.

Our performance indicators have improved. – Credit memos are down. While we pursued this model, we have reduced the quantity of

- Have procedures where none existed before.

- Everyone speaking the same language.

- We have consistency in operation...
  not dependent upon any one individual.

- There is a home for good ideas.

- The system is universal within the company.

- Have formalized the corrective action process.

- Our performance indicators are revealing highly positive results.

- Reduced product rework.

- We have early detection of potential design oversights.

- Improved team communications.

- Increased participation in design reviews.

Figure 4.13 TQM and ISO 9000 benefits as described by employees.

credits being written by 70%. A credit is the result of a mistake. This represents a saving of $200 to $300 for both Foxboro and our customers on each credit memo issued.

Improved team communication. – Employees know what is expected of them and this removes or reduces the defensiveness or squabbles that seemed to go along with events and ownership.

Increased participation in design reviews. – Employees now come to the meetings prepared and understand the expected outcomes of the meetings. The result of this process streamlining has surprised us. A significant event occurred after the process had been in place that validated the efforts. Our engineering staff took three multilayer printed circuit board schematics from drawings to working prototypes (multilayer board and surface mount components) onto a single panel with fully functional test points in two weeks, versus the more typical four to six months. If the requirement is speed, all involved employees simultaneously using practiced routines is the answer.

A safer work environment – One of our valued customers pointed out that they used to say "Safety is number 1," but they noticed that after some initial improvement, their results leveled off. When they switched to "Quality is number 1," they achieved a new level of excellence. We experienced the same. Employees can get injured when they are doing something they haven't been trained in. ISO 9000 requires that employees are trained for and understand their roles. With the work associated with ISO 9000 and help from our insurance company, we were able to dramatically reduce injuries as seen in Figure 4.14.

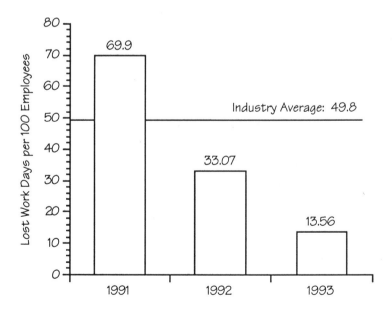

4.14 *Foxboro's ISO 9000 efforts contributed to a dramatic improvement in work place safety as expressed by lost work days per 100 employees.*

Beyond ISO 9000

ISO 9000 was certainly a significant event in the history of the Foxboro Company. In addition to the certificate, we achieved the objectives we set for process improvements and further improving our business methodologies.

With continuous improvement being one of our TQM cornerstones, we quickly evaluated what the next step in our journey should be, now that we had achieved strategic alignment with ISO 9000. We concluded that the Baldrige application was a future possibility. Its criteria provides an excellent means for evaluating our performance and provides a foundation for improvement. At about the same time, we learned that the state of Massachusetts had initiated the Armand Feigenbaum Massachusetts Quality Award based on the Baldrige criteria. We viewed the Massachusetts Quality Award as a good opportunity to do a "dry run" of the Baldrige and simultaneously take the next step in the journey. A year after receiving our ISO 9001 certification and after many hours of preparation, we submitted our application for the award. A rigorous audit and six months later, we became one of the proud recipients of the first Armand Feigenbaum Massachusetts Quality Award in October of 1992 (see Figure 4.15).

4.15 Foxboro's TQM efforts enabled it to win the Armand Feigenbaum Massachusetts Quality Award based on the Baldrige criteria.

Coincidentally, in October 1992, Foxboro was selected by *Industry Week* as having one of the top 10 plants in the U.S. as a part of their annual Best Plants awards (see Figure 4.16). In 1993, this same plant won the prestigious CASA/SME L.E.A.D. Award for Leadership and Excellence in the Application and Development of Computer Integrated Manufacturing. The award is given by the Computer and Automated Systems Association of the Society of Manufacturing Engineers (CASA/ SME). The recognition we have received through these awards provides benchmarks demonstrating that our pursuit of TQM, built on a strong ISO 9000 foundation, is on course.

The Bottom Line Is the Bottom Line

Our customers saw what we were doing and wanted to share in our methodologies and results. For example, we used a Foxboro QIP team with a team from an AMOCO operation. Through our joint efforts, we became the first certified "Distributed Controls" supplier for their

4.16 *Foxboro's ISO 9001 certification and its TQM programs contributed to* Industry Week *recognizing it as one of the top 10 plants in the U.S.*

Chocolate Bayou plant. While the team was one of the activities most visible to AMOCO, it was really the entire company coming together, as well as our distributors (Figure 4.17).

Our customers have responded favorably through their growing commitment to our products and services. For example, while pulp and paper industry capital expenditures plummeted from roughly $17 billion to $12 billion between 1990 and 1991, our volume in this market grew by more than 15%!

This is what it is all about — helping our customers become more competitive by helping them directly — assisting them as they improve their process with our products and services, and sharing with them common challenges such as ISO 9000. Hopefully, we are saving them hundreds of hours so they can better serve their customers. Of course, that will mean more business for them and for us.

**THE FOXBORO COMPANY
FOXBORO, MASSACHUSETTS**

IN RECOGNITION OF
THE ESTABLISHMENT OF
OUR QUALITY PARTNERSHIP.
BASED UPON SUSTAINED PERFORMANCE,
CONFORMANCE TO REQUIREMENTS,
DEMONSTRATED COMMITMENT,
AND CONTINUOUS IMPROVEMENT

AMOCO CHEMICAL COMPANY
CHOCOLATE BAYOU PLANT
ALVIN, TEXAS

HONORS THE FOXBORO COMPANY AS A
CERTIFIED QUALITY SUPPLIER ON OCTO-
BER 11, 1990

4.17 Through the efforts of a joint QIP team with AMOCO, Foxboro became the first company to achieve certified status for the supply of automation systems to the Chocolate Bayou Plant.

Pulp and Paper Industry Seminar

The Why's and How's of ISO 9000 Certification

Foxboro Welcomes

Weyerhaeuser

Continuous Improvement...
From Fiberline to Bottom Line

4.18 To help with their ISO 9000 pursuits, Foxboro provides regular training sessions for both its customers and suppliers.

To help with their ISO 9000 pursuits, we hold regular training sessions for both our customers and suppliers (Figure 4.18). We average two to three customer training sessions per month. Additionally, in 1993 Foxboro sponsored 12 regional training sessions to promote ISO 9000 development. We know they appreciate our efforts — we are using our quality organization to meet our definition of quality: "To exceed our customers expectations while maintaining profitable growth."

5

How Will We Ever Be Ready In Time?

Qualifying for and receiving certification is an enterprisewide endeavor. Even with management commitment and an existing quality infrastructure in place, it can take anywhere from three months to one year to mobilize your operations and get the proper documents, procedures, internal audits, and practices in place.

This chapter presents a sample project schedule and describes the events leading up to a certification audit, based on the experiences of the Foxboro Company.

How Long Will It Take?

The following time frames for certification are suggested; they assume a single plant operation and management commitment.

3 to 6 months	If you are in full compliance to a military standard, G.M.P., or nuclear standard.
6 to 10 months	If your organization has fairly up-to-date procedures, job descriptions, and a working quality organization.
10 to 18 months	If the organization has only sketchy procedures and its records are haphazard. Your quality organization is still responsible for final inspection, and still takes the blame for the substandard product shipped. If you have a very large plant site.

| 18 to 24 months | If you still don't have full commitment from senior management. You shouldn't begin your countdown until your management commits to pursuing certification. |

A study reported by *Quality Systems Update* indicates that companies with quality systems that require little change achieve certification in 8.5 months on average. Companies that must make large modifications to their quality systems or do not have a quality system in place obtain certification in 13.5 months on average.

Most operations are focused on immediate problems, such as revenue and profits. Our survey of companies that achieved ISO 9000 early indicates that until there is a "stake" in the ground and people can see it coming, little motivation exists and the experience can be very frustrating for those trying to generate any meaningful effort.

The next section contains 14 steps that will enable you to measure your progress, as well as to estimate when you will be able to entertain the auditors with a world-class operation that is fully compliant with ISO 9000. A sample project schedule is illustrated in Figure 5.1.

How Much Will It Cost?

The cost of ISO 9000 compliance depends on the existing condition of your organization. Most certified companies have not tracked the costs. As discussed earlier, the value to the business far outweighs the cost, so tracking these costs is a nonvalue-added activity as long as your operation stays within its planned operating budget. One company's postaudit study showed a nine-month return on investment. Again it is a function of your current status, but the greater the opportunity for improvement, the greater the opportunity for return.

A survey of ISO 9000 certified U.S. companies was completed in the fall of 1993 by Quality Systems Update (QSU) and Deloitte & Touche. Of the 1679 surveys sent, an unusually high 620 responses were received. The results were reported in QSU's Fall 1993 special report, "Registered

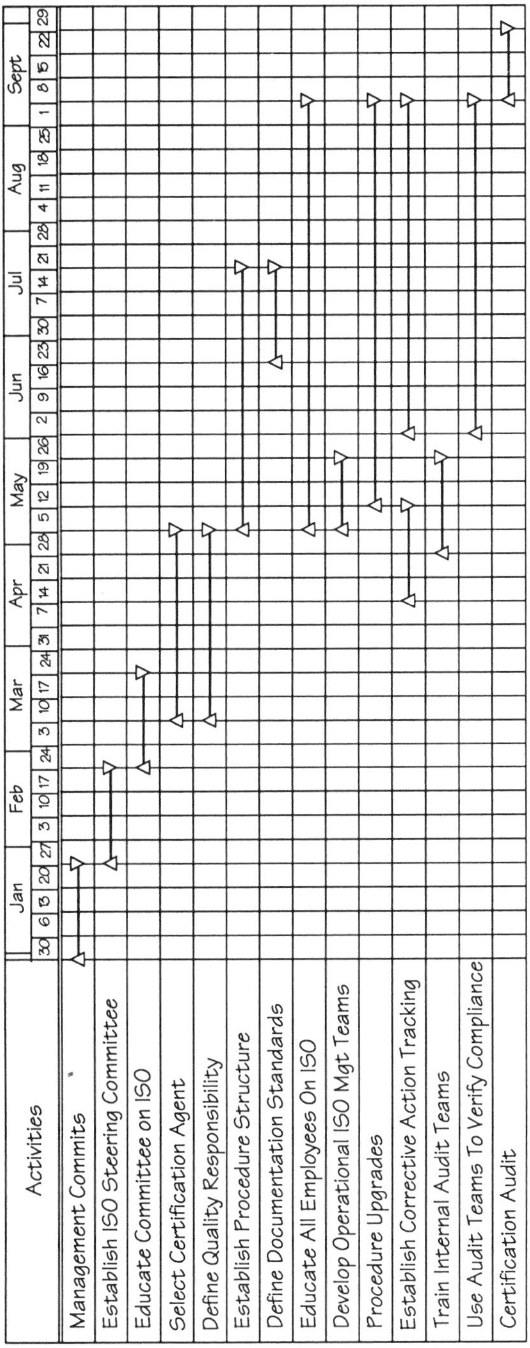

Figure 5.1 Sample project schedule illustrating the major steps undertaken by The Foxboro Company to achieve certification.

Companies Report Big Savings", as well as in Business Week's November 1,1993 issue, "More Than A Passport to European Business: Most U.S. outfits meeting ISO 9000 rules find paybacks galore."

The survey results were both surprising and expected. One surprise was that only about 50% of those companies surveyed felt they had achieved a payback of less than three years on their investment. The survey also asked several other questions regarding the reasons for pursuing ISO 9000 certification, its effects, and the respondents future intentions. A correlation analysis between these responses and the stated payback demonstrates some of the lessons to be learned. Highlights of the survey conclusions follow.

When asked why they pursued registration, "requirements of EC regulations were cited more often (27.1% vs. 16.7) by companies that did not realize tangible benefits within 3.3 years. Further, these same companies mentioned quality benefits less frequently (50.2%), than did those indicating swift and measurable returns (70.3%). This would imply a correlation between registration motivation and payback."

When queried about the most significant external benefit (response by the market), the following prioritized benefits were reported, higher perceived quality (76.3%), competitive edge (68.5%), improved customer satisfaction (66.1%), and reduced customer quality audits (41.1%). Improved customer satisfaction was cited by 73.2% of respondents reporting a payback of less than 3 years and by 57.5% of those with a longer payback.

When asked about internal returns, those companies claiming a payback of less than 3 years cited reduced scrap/rework at nearly twice the rate (30.1%) as those who reported a longer payback (15.5). "These dramatic differences call into question whether companies with delayed returns used ISO 9000 as a vehicle for making significant improvements to the business or for the sole purpose of becoming registered."

These results indicate that companies using ISO 9000 as a quality improvement opportunity have better results and a faster payback.

When Foxboro's plant managers were first told of the plan for the upgrade of the procedures, you can imagine it was not widely welcomed. Their first question was, "Where is the budget and what is the account number to dump these costs into?" The vice-president of manufacturing recognized this activity as part of running a good business and responded by saying, "Don't ask for something that you should have been doing already. If you can't get the QC engineers to participate, we will get new engineers. If you can't get the supervision to participate, we will get new supervision. If I can't get my plant managers to participate," he stopped there and looked around the room and continued, "Need I say any more?" That took care of the cost issues as well as senior-level commitment.

The 14 Steps

The following is a description of the process that will help you achieve compliance and certification quickly. This is one approach. You should try to create your own plan tailored to your situation.

1 • Senior Management Commits – The old adage that commitment must come from the top holds true. Senior management must commit to achieving ISO 9000 compliance with a firm determination to achieve the objective, allocate the necessary resources, and assign responsibility appropriately. ISO 9000 is an enterprisewide standard that requires the shared commitment and involvement of all the executives within the senior management group and their respective operations. Remember this is not a "free lunch"; sacrifice is required for this commitment. Your organization has two choices: It can fund an outside consultant with a staff of writers or it can slow down other projects and perform the task with internal people who are close to the process and can usually do a much better job than an outsider. Should you decide to go internally, your management must keep in mind during the process that this is not business as usual; a strong commitment is needed.

At Foxboro, we let our employees and supervisors determine what would slow down. As long as it did not interfere with delivery integrity, their recommendation was generally accepted. Their only requirement was to tell us what would give.

Once you have senior management commitment, actively use it. Ask your plant managers to put ISO 9000 at the top of each staff meeting. This way it will not get lost in the agenda, and putting it first will send a clear message to the staff. Declare your intentions throughout the entire organization, with a letter of commitment from the senior person in the organization. That commitment will serve you well, and, without it, your chances for success are significantly reduced.

2 • Establish an ISO 9000 Steering Council – The primary charter of this council is to establish a comprehensive ISO 9000 development program and ensure its implementation with the proper allocation of resources. This group functions as the focal point for all the activities within the organization related to ISO 9000. They will provide the comprehensive assessments necessary for scheduling and supporting the audit. They will be negotiating tasks and interfaces within their own organization as the project leaders, as well as between organizations for linkages.

Recognize that ISO 9000 is an enterprisewide effort when putting this council together, and that everyone must be involved. Even if you are preparing for ISO 9002, be sure to include representatives from all organizations that intersect the certified areas. When you go to your senior management for representatives, ask for the best. Remind them that these people will be representing them and committing their organizations to plans of action. Remind them that they do not want to be the organizational group that causes the company to fail (that reminder seems to be effective in areas that are not completely committed). Make sure the people assigned to the committee are your best performers. Although it seems that they can't be spared for the task, you need the best. Once they are on the team, remind their managers that this is not a free ride — they should work with their designate to free up some of his or her time and see that recognition is received for this work. With the good performers on your team, you will notice that they receive peer support that will make accomplishment of the overall mission easier. One of the first tasks should be the education of the council.

*3 • **Educate the Council on ISO 9000*** – It is critical that the council members understand ISO 9000 and its elements in detail, as they will champion the effort in their respective organizations. It is also important that they develop a consensus among themselves as to what ISO 9000 is within their organization. To assist in their efforts, questionnaires developed by the various certifying agencies should be obtained and used to assess organizational readiness. The education of the steering committee will create a group of roving experts, who are also self-reinforcing drivers with the ability to move the process forward quickly. People generally don't want to put work into something for which they don't understand the reason, especially if they would rather be doing something else. If your team can convey the purpose of the effort and provide correct and timely answers to questions, they will motivate the other employees to join the effort. Conversely, not providing answers will stall the effort.

*4 • **Evaluate and Select a Certification Agent*** – The evaluation and selection of a certification agent is critical and should be viewed as a marriage between two parties. Thus, you will want to look very closely at the likely partners. The following is a checklist of things to consider when you go through your search for a certification partner:

- Your certification audit should not be the first time you meet your auditors. Plan on spending some time "courting" your auditors.
- Does this potential partner need to carry a recognized European registration mark?
- Is the potential partner local or will this be a long-distance relationship? Don't dismiss a long-distance relationship if the partner seems right, but involves an extra cost. Try to find out what the costs are, including their application fees, initial visit costs, the certification audit costs and expenses, cost of future get togethers, and cancellation fees.
- Is the potential partner your type? Do they know about your type of business, and can they talk your language? Do you have the same interests (authorized to grant certification to your type of business),

have they worked with other people in your line of business, and can they give you a reference in your industry to call?

- What kind of friends does the agency keep? Do they have MOU's (Memorandums of Understanding) with other registration organizations that recognize the others' certification, for example, UL and BSI. Be careful as there are different levels of MOU's. The following are four common MOU's.[1]
  - A *Bilateral Agreement* says we unconditionally accept the other's certificate .
  - A *Full MOU* means we still accept the other's certificate, but every so often we would like to view the audits.
  - A *Developing MOU* means that we have agreed to look at each other very closely and may honor each other's certificate in the future.
  - A *Base MOU* means that we have agreed to agree at some time in the future.

  When the agent's MOU claims sound too good to be true, they are. Ask for details and type. Clearly the more the better, but don't discount them if they only have a few.
- Is the agency available? When you call, do they speak with you or pass you around? Do they meet the 48-hour return-your-call test? Can they meet with you for an introductory chat? Can they specify when they could perform the certification audit?
- Is the agency expensive? Don't be misled by an artificially low initial quote with the intention of accelerating the meter later. They are all fairly competitive; however, be leery of the "two people, two days" quote. Respect the person who might want to go to a place where you can talk and enjoy yourselves; that's how good relationships are built.
- Now, for the most important question: Do you like each other? Do they approach you with a positive attitude — one that indicates they want to make it a positive experience for both, that they are really interested in your making the grade? They realize that you may be a bit nervous and are open and patient with your exploring questions, and they respond quickly and accurately to your inquiries.

---

[1] Catherine Neville, General Manager, QMI.

Your questions may be similar to the following ones:

How often will you stop by and visit? Some certifiers visit every six months, others only once a year. There are advantages and disadvantages either way.

How long in advance will you call before you come? Some certifiers lay out a three-year schedule and allow you to look and be your best when they get there. Others call only two weeks before they plan to arrive. While this can be very uncomfortable, especially if you have a busy schedule or a full house of customers, it is palatable, but rarely can you look and feel your best. Don't assume that you can only spruce up just before they get there — they know how to get an accurate reading regardless of your preparation.

How do they look at the world? Some certifiers only see black or white, pass or fail, when they score you after the certification audit. Others see shades of passing or failing and give a range of scores. They will all ask the same kinds of questions and look in the same 400 places if you are going after ISO 9001. Our evaluation considered the "pass/fail" approach undesirable. We wanted to know how we were doing for two reasons:

1. We wanted to use this as an exercise for improvement and would first focus on our weaker areas. Pass/fail would not provide that information.

2. If we didn't know where we were marginal, it was unlikely that we would discover it prior to their next audit. The auditors are likely to look first where the result on the last audit was marginal.

What if we don't pass on the first try of the certification audit? It depends on how badly you missed the points and where. Each certifier has a different approach. One may say, "we will be back within 30 days" and then will only look at your shortfalls, provided they weren't major points. At the other extreme, another may say, "don't hold your breath," meaning that you're back to square one. Ask, and be sure to negotiate a follow-up date once you have set up the agreement for the first audit, just in case you don't make it the first time.

What's the family like? Are the siblings capable of being quiet about what they might overhear; how can you be sure? You want to make sure that the registrar has confidentiality agreements with its employees and all who would see your audit information.

ISO 9000 is an interpretive standard and, therefore, has gray areas. Try to find a certification agent that understands your business. Get to know the probable lead auditor and find out the interpretation of some of the questions that you might not be able to resolve. This will allow you to calibrate your initial approach to the lead auditor's expectations. In addition, make it clear to your agency that you want someone who knows your industry's practices and "common sense."

Confirm that your certifier is financially sound, and scout out how their auditors were trained and who they work for. Some registrars actually out-source the audits to independent agencies, and you have to ask yourself whether that is in your best interest. You also want to make sure the auditors have been trained to a standard such as ASQC's Certified Program for Auditors of Quality systems.

If I should pass the certification audit, how can I announce it to the world? You need to find out not only exactly how you can inform your customers, but how they will be informing other certification agencies. In most cases, you are placed in a registry where customers and competitors alike can look you up. Hopefully, it is easily accessible. Your registrar should also have your announcement placed in directories like the *Quality Systems Update, Registered Company Directory for the United States and Canada*, as discussed in the previous chapter.

5 • *Define Quality Responsibility* – After the ISO Steering Council has been educated, begin the process of clearly defining the responsibility for quality and the associated processes, from the president down through the entire organization. The definition of responsibility does not necessarily indicate that the individual has to be dedicated solely to quality full time; however, it does mean the organization has to demonstrate that an individual is actively involved in the quality management of a particular process and has that specific responsibility.

This includes documented proof that there has been an activity associated with the defined responsibility. This may sound fairly easy and, surprisingly, it is. Start by laying out a rough flow chart of your organization with your steering council, and then have each of the ISO 9000 team's members identify where their organization is affected by the standard. After they determine their areas of responsibility, have them sit with the other members for a review. You might discover that you're responsible for more than you think, or that some people think they have responsibilities that you think you have, or that no one has responsibility for certain areas. In any case, this can have ramifications beyond the scope of your council. If so, don't mess around, go to the top, explain your problem, ask for direction, and make it clear why it is so critical. Also ask for a decision date. This exercise accomplishes two tasks:

1. It becomes the basis for beginning your quality manual.
2. It is a basic step in defining how your organization satisfies its customers — you now know who is doing what.

To assist the auditors, you will want to create an organization chart that will support your definition of how the responsibility flows. This will become the basis for your corporate-level quality manual and probably looks just like your current organization chart (just be sure the titles match your description of those responsible).

6 • Establish Procedure Structure – Before you start writing procedures, your group should determine the format of the procedures, as well as the best and most efficient method for maintaining this structure once it is established. This structure is the area that will require the greatest effort in preparation for the audit, and it will have a significant impact on your long-term procedural maintenance efficiency, so it deserves significant thought and effort. The system you design should allow maximum flexibility at the lowest cost.

A possible strategy would be to develop three (or two for a single plant) layers of procedures. A few, relatively stable procedures reside at the top of this structure, and the vast number of dynamic procedures reside at the lower levels. This approach minimizes the number of procedures and dramatically reduces the maintenance and coordination requirements.

In this layered structure, as seen in Figure 5.2, the top or corporate level is relatively general and primarily focused on the various standards that are being supported, how to approach ISO 9000 requirements, and the definition of the corporate quality assurance responsibilities. It should be brief.

The next level would cover plant or group-level procedures. They would define common elements and practices stated at the corporate level, and describe in greater detail the elements that relate to them.

The third and final level, departmental operations, is where detailed procedures, documents, and records are maintained. The majority of the detailed procedures reside at this level as well as in the department where they are being used.

It is likely that your existing quality procedures will need to be restructured. At a minimum, you will need to reference these procedures to the specific elements of the ISO 9000 standard to which they relate.

There is no one correct method for writing the actual procedure. We recommend that you allow each organization to generate the procedures in the fashion with which they are most comfortable. The steering committee should set a framework for minimum requirements of contents, and then let the groups decide what works best for them. The framework should require at least a date of issuance, revision number, location for use, an ISO 9000 reference number, and a procedure name. Acceptable procedures that are already in place can be used, as long as it can be ensured that they meet the framework. Procedures can take many forms. Most often, we see a playscript format. Sometimes a flow chart format works the best. They can be in an electronic database or in paper form. They can be on the backs of material transfer forms. They can be signs on the wall or even copies of the operating instructions that came with the equipment with an added cover page for control. Let the groups be creative in how they solve *their* problem. For example, one of our groups took pictures at each station of an assembly line, attached them to sheets of paper on which the operator wrote descriptive comments, and put them together to form the procedure for the line. The more hurdles you put in front of them, the slower their progress will be.

As these procedures are being written, opportunities for standardization and replication in common areas shouldn't be missed. You will

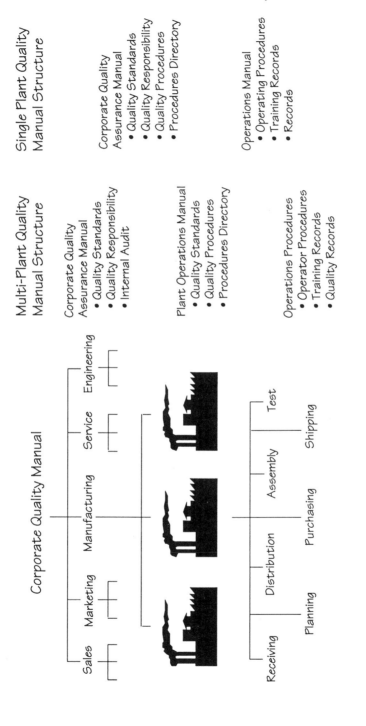

Figure 5.2 Example of a hierarchial procedure structure used by The Foxboro Company.

want to establish a structure that can readily uncover these common areas before beginning, and avoid a lot of unnecessary duplication. One strategy is to define general procedures simply and then break out only the necessary details according to the organizations they represent. This way, procedures will be relatively general at the higher levels and only get into detail as required at the lower levels.

You will also want to establish measures for progress. The number of outstanding procedures to be written is one measure that you can suggest to the groups as an indicator of progress. Before you get started, you will also need to define other requirements to ensure that the procedures incorporate all the critical ISO 9000 requirements.

7 • Define Documentation Standards – In this phase, the steering council must define and clarify all the documents required from their operations to satisfy the ISO 9000 standard. They should also identify as many of the commonly used documents as possible to save work for the organization.

Divide the documents that need to be defined and proceduralized among the team members to work on. Then prototype these documents in a single area and once the problems are removed, get the council to endorse them. Have each member go out to his or her area and do the installation. They may make their own adjustments, and that's OK, as long as they stay within the framework and document it to meet the standard. Attempt to make one document serve as many purposes as possible. You will need controlled procedures that will address all of the elements of the standard. The challenge is to identify and generate them and to then ensure that your employees follow them.

The following is a listing of the records that must be generated and maintained to support the standard.

Documentation

• Quality Policy	4.1.1
• Responsibility & Authority	4.1.2.1
• Quality Manual	4.2.1
• Quality System Procedures	4.2.2
(Included or reference in manual)	

- Quality Plan   4.2.3
- Contract Review   4.3.1
- Contract Requirements   4.3.2
- Design Control   4.4.1
- Design Planning   4.4.2
- Organizational and Technical Interfaces   4.4.3
- Design Input   4.4.4
- Design Output   4.4.5
- Design Changes   4.4.7
- Document and Data Control   4.5.1
- Master Listing   4.5.2
- Purchasing   4.6.1
- Product Identification and Traceability   4.8
- Work Instructions   4.9
- Inspection and Testing   4.10.1
- Calibration Control   4.11.1
- Calibration Procedures   4.11.2.C
- ReInspections due to Calibration Failure   4.11.2.F
- Nonconforming Products   4.13.1
- Review of Nonconforming Products   4.13.2
- Repair/Rework Procedures   4.13.2
- Corrective Actions   4.14
- Preventive Actions   4.14
- Handling, Storage, Packaging,   4.15.1
  Preservation and Delivery
- Quality Records   4.16
- Internal Audits   4.17
- Identification of Training Needs   4.18
- Service   4.19
- Statistical Techniques   4.20

Records Required
- Management Review   4.11
- Contract Review   4.3.4
- Design Review   4.4.5

- Design Verification   4.4.7
- Design Validation   4.4.8
- Sub-Contractors Evaluation   4.6.2
- Damaged or Lost Customer Supplied Product   4.7
- Traceability when required   4.8
- Qualified Processes, Equipment and Personnel   4.9
- Urgent Product Releases (as required)   4.10.2.3
- Inspection and Test Records   4.10.4
- Test Equipment/Software Conformance Status   4.11.1
- Reinspection due to Calibration Failure   4.11.2.F
- Nonconforming Product disposition   4.13.2
- Root Cause Analysis for Corrective Action   4.14.2.B
- Procedural Changes from Preventive Action   4.14.3.D
- Results of Internal Audits   4.17
- Training   4.18

Because it is your business, the standard must be interpreted according to how you conduct your operations. For example, a company that sells catalog items will maintain a different set of contract records than one that builds nuclear power plants. Assembly documentation doesn't have to be a drawing; it can be a photo or a prototype with a part number written on it. The only requirement is that you control these drawings/photos/models to ensure that the proper item is being built at the right time and being tested properly.

It is impossible in the space of this book to cover all the conceivable methods for addressing these requirements. We would, however, like to briefly cover a few of the items here that won't be addressed later:

Quality Manual – The quality manual represents the focal point for your plan to run the business. Consider making this manual as "auditor friendly" as possible. The easiest approach would be to construct your manual(s) in the ISO 9000 format, that is, with the same section order and the same contents being addressed as the standard. Consider a multilevel approach to your manual as described for procedures. And remember that the more you write, the more they have to audit.

Two examples of the contents of a corporate-level manual are shown in Figure 5.3 and Figure 5.4. The first is "auditor friendly," and the second is less friendly and addresses the standard in a more indirect way. Both documents address the elements of the standard superbly. In the latter, outsiders (your potential customers as well as the auditors) will have a more difficult time finding how you cover each area. Why is this important? The American National Standards Institute (ANSI) has now made the ISO 9000 standard the national standard by which most current and future audits will be conducted. If you have a manual such as the less friendly one shown, consider creating a conversion index to help the auditors. This could be messy if you are splitting up multiple sections to address each ISO 9000 section, but it is better to plan in advance through the use of this conversion document than to wait until the auditors arrive for the documentation review.

At the second tier of your manuals, again try to stay within the constructs of the standard. Both the "auditor friendly" corporate-level manual and the second tier should be aligned to the standard. Starting with an effective manual is the first step in having a good audit, and more important, it demonstrates that you understand your business.

Training Records – We all live with the fear that some untrained rookie will come and repair our car's brakes, the plane's landing gear, or the control system of a nuclear power plant. The people who put our products together and take our orders need training (at Foxboro we do the nuclear power plants). ISO 9000 requires that training occurs and that it is reasonable for the given task. The proof the auditors are looking for is the training record that is maintained for every important task affecting the product. Certainly, you won't need a training record on how to open a door, but you will need records to show that the employees know how to operate the equipment associated with the product, that they have been trained on the assembly process, and, in all cases, how they can differentiate between good and bad workmanship. As you go through your procedure development, you will identify those tasks that affect the product, and from there you will be able to systematically identify the education and training needed for the job.

TABLE OF CONTENTS

Figure 5.3 An example of an "auditor friendly" table of contents from a corporate-level quality manual.

TABLE OF CONTENTS

Section	Title	Page
SP	Statement of Policy	SP-1
TC	Table of Contents	TC-1
S	Scope	S-1
	1.1 Departmental Responsibilities	S-3
	1.2 Company Organization	S-10
	1.3 Applicable Documents	S-18
TD	Terms and Definitions	TD-1
1	Contract Administration	1-1
	1.1 Customer Order Control	1-1
2	Quality Records	2-1
	2.1 Quality System Documentation	2-1
	2.2 Records	2-2
	2.3 Stamp Control	2-3
	2.4 Certification	2-4
3	Quality Performance/Cost Reporting	3-1
	3.1 Quality Related Cost Disposition	3-1
	3.2 Product Performance Reports	3-3
4	Procurement	4-1
	4.1 Purchase Order Control	4-1
	4.2 Approved Vendor Requirements	4-4

Figure 5.4 An example of an "auditor unfriendly" table of contents from a corporate-level quality manual.

A generic training record developed by the ISO Steering Committee is shown in Figure 5.5. Prior to completing the training records, the supervisors would sit down with a group of employees performing the job and together identify what was required to perform the task. They would then create a checklist of the key attributes for which training should occur and later confirm the employees' capability. At the end of this exercise, each employee performing this task will have a training record generated with the supervisor signed off on the employee's ability to perform the task prior to his or her being left alone on the job.

It is likely that as you are starting this ISO 9000 readiness activity, you do not have a training record for everyone who is performing jobs for which such a record would be appropriate. In this case, a retroactive training record is acceptable, as long as you specify this is a one-time start-up policy. When Foxboro was audited, it was noted that there was quite a bit of "wet ink" on the documents. That was acceptable because the activities complied with the current procedures and the appropriate records were in place and demonstrated a "reasonable period of compliance." What is a reasonable period? If you can't decide, ask your auditor, as each situation is different. While you may make it through the first audit, remember that the auditors will return in six months and will be looking for the records of new employees in the department. These records will need to conform to the new employee's starting date.

Occasionally, a job will be defined as requiring a degree. You may have people in the job who do not have a degree. Make sure you have a procedure in place to allow capable nongraduates to comply with your requirements. Define a process for waiving the requirement and show the evaluation methods with a checklist.

Finally, the training records should be readily accessible to the supervisors, who are responsible for the record's accuracy and utilization. It is usually prudent to keep the records in the work areas and also possibly having the employees maintaining their own set. Some operations have determined that the records are to be maintained in the personnel files. If this is the case, consider two personnel files, as a number of employees consider it an invasion of privacy when an auditor or outsider goes through their personnel file.

When you let your employees maintain their own training records, you will discover they take an interest in them and will generally ensure they are accurate. The better employees will also seek additional training and want to keep growing — this is a win-win situation.

PERSONNEL TRAINING RECORD			
Name	Dept. #		
Title			
Education			
Formal Training			
Work Experience/On-the-Job Training			
Employee's Signature			
Supervisor's Signature			
Date			

Note: The better the training record is, the fewer the instructions that will be required in the procedures. Also, don't forget that you will need a documented procedure on how you will go about defining training needs (4.18).

Figure 5.5 A sample training record.

8 • Educate All Employees On ISO 9000 – It takes a long time and repeated communications to get any message out to all corners of your organization. It is also essential that everyone comprehends the meaning and requirements of ISO 9000 as it requires the full participation of all employees. When you let everyone know why you are introducing an experience possibly perceived as painful, it will reduce the resistance to change and will gain support for continued compliance. This can be done by educating all employees through an employee newsletter, as seen in Figure 5.6, and involving the clear support of the senior member of the organization.

When employees understand the requirements and why it is important to the company, they are less reluctant and do a better job. Through education, employees are mentally prepared for the very exhaustive preparation and audit. This preparation leads to confidence, which is apparent when they meet with the auditors.

Ongoing education also includes training your employees on how to deal with the auditors and how to respond to their questions. The education process extends over several months and requires multiple communications before the general population understands what ISO 9000 is all about. During this phase, continue to communicate the company's quality policy, as this will be part of the auditor's inquiry. You might also consider posting your quality policy every 60 meters and be confident that sooner or later the message will get through.

Keeping the management abreast of the organization's progress will also help the cause. By posting your progress measures, broken down by organization, you will ensure that those falling behind will receive the appropriate peer pressure (no senior manager wants their organization to be the reason for the company not being ready). About a month before the audit, you might want the supervision to hold group meetings across the company for final preparation and to answer final questions.

9 • Develop Operational ISO 9000 Management Teams – With the education of the ISO 9000 Steering Council and the preparation of all the documents and procedures, it becomes necessary to develop vehicles by which this information can be introduced into the organization and

OnCourse

Premier Edition

ISO 9001 Update

A Quality Improvement Newsletter for Employees of The Foxboro Company   **January 1991**

Total Quality is the Goal

Consistent with our pursuit of **total quality** at The Foxboro Company, we are in the process of becoming ISO 9001 certified. Achieving certification by late February will make Foxboro one of the first major US manufacturers to become certified across all its manufacturing facilities. Not only will this provide Foxboro with a competitive advantage, but it will also demonstrate to our customers that our business processes satisfy the requirements of the internationally accepted quality standard, ISO 9001.

Virtually every operation in the company is involved in the certification process and associated audits. Your management team strongly supports this activity and we appreciate the efforts of those directly involved in achieving this important goal.

S. S. Shaffran

ISO 9001: What is it?

ISO 9001 is one of the business quality standards which make up the ISO 9000 series. Certification demonstrates the capability of a supplier to control the processes that determine the acceptability of the product or service being supplied. The standards were

> **"As the international standard for quality systems, ISO 9000 serves to attest that the accredited supplier can demonstrate the ability to control the processes that determine the acceptability of the product."**

developed by the International Standards Organization (ISO), the international agency for standardization, headquartered in Geneva, Switzerland.

The International Standards Organization is composed of national standards bodies from 91 countries. The United States is represented in the ISO by the American National Standards Institute (ANSI). ANSI is composed of more than 250 US organizations and has historically determined the standards within the US. The American Society for Quality Control (ASQC) is a leading member of ANSI.

The ISO 9000 document is composed of a series quality standards that address different aspects of the business process. Firms will pursue certification for one of the standards listed below according to the their type of business.

ISO 9001- Confirms conformance to specified requirements during design, development, production, test installation and servicing.

ISO 9002- is used only when production, installation and servicing are needing conformance confirmation.

ISO 9003- is the least detailed

standard and requires conformance only in final test and inspection.

ISO 9004- contains guidance on technical, administrative and human factors affecting the quality of products and services. This standard is for internal use only and not to be used in contractual or certification situations.

ISO 9001 is a quality standard for the business process and not a certification for product reliability such as a "UL" approval.

What ISO 9001 Is Not

ISO 9001 is a generic standard and represents a minimum requirement for an effective quality system. By comparison, the Nuclear 10cfr50 and the Good Manufacturing Practices Criteria are more focused and require a higher level of commitment in certain areas. ISO 9000 does not tell you how to document your system, nor does it define what a Quality Manual is, or define what a quality plan is or what is an adequate Quality Policy.

Mr. Juran has pointed out that ISO 9000 provides no provision for continuous improvement, nor does it

FOXBORO
A SIEBE COMPANY

Figure 5.6 Internal newsletter educates employees on ISO 9000.

the momentum established to execute the various elements of the program. This can be accomplished by members of the ISO 9000 Steering Council setting up operational units within their own organizations, usually by department, educating them, and then going about installing the ISO 9000 elements that are relevant to that group. Figure 5.7 illustrates how this was accomplished through the use of matrixed task teams at Foxboro.

The ISO 9000 Management Team members, once educated, act as the resident experts. When questions come up that they are unable to address, or do not feel comfortable with, the issues are brought to the ISO 9000 Steering Council. The ISO 9000 Steering Council develops a position or contacts the lead auditor of the certification agency for a disposition. The ISO 9000 Management Teams should consist of senior members of the various organizations with key supervisors from each group. Their primary tasks should encompass at least the following:

• Defining the flow within their organizations that will determine the areas affected by ISO 9000 (use flow charts). Reconcile duties at intersection points.
• Administer the progress measures.
• Assume responsibility for their area's conformance.

The compliance process should be managed on a weekly basis with the appropriate indicators in place to support visibility. In reality, this is when the project really gets its wings and develops a personality of its own. Encourage people to get involved and use the management-by-walking-around technique. There will be those who aggressively ask questions; answer them quickly. But don't assume that because some people aren't asking questions, all is well. In the beginning, they are most likely assimilating the changes and new requirements.

10 • Procedure Upgrades – Procedure upgrades will probably occur at all levels of the organization and in some cases this can involve an enormous amount of work. For most companies these procedures, more often then not, belong to the quality or industrial engineering departments, neither

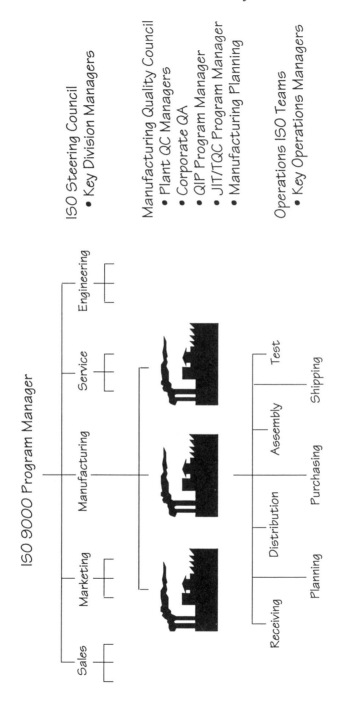

Figure 5.7 Matrixed task teams assist in ISO 9000 audit preparation.

of which is staffed to support the load required to bring procedures up to compliance. While you may have procedures in place, in some areas they may be written one way whereas the job is performed in an entirely different manner — this is quite common.

If you have effectively deployed your operational ISO 9000 teams, they have identified the major informational flows and understand the documentation and record requirements. They have been able to identify where procedures are required. It's at this point that you should bring the real power of ISO 9000 to bear — the employees. The employees are the ones who know the actual task better than anyone else in your organization. Consider having them create the procedures. If you allow them to do this, you will enjoy the following benefits as we did at Foxboro:

• A potentially enormous work load is spread over a large group of employees rather than a few. This will ensure a shorter duration of the activity.
• The most qualified and most knowledgeable individuals will write the procedures ensuring that the practices align with the document.
• The employees will be made part of the process and feel like part of a team that is striving for the same common goal. You might even hear statements like "the company is finally starting to listen to us!"

Some in your organization may question the ability of their employees to write procedures, and in some areas they might be correct, but with a little help from their supervisors, most employees can draft a box and diamond flow chart. You can even write it up into a playscript format later, but that isn't necessary. A sample of a simple procedure is illustrated in Figure 5.8.

Once you have the draft procedure ready, have it reviewed by all the employees who perform the task. You might discover that they all don't agree. Treat this as an opportunity for a small group to go out and figure out the best of all worlds. We have a documented case where the yields in one of our areas showed a dramatic increase because of this exercise. Once the mini-team has come up with the best method, have all the employees sign the procedures. Not only will you have a training record

Sample Procedure   Procedure # _____ Revision ____
                      Date Issued ___/___/___
                      Ref. ISO 9000 Standard _____
                      Department _____

Title | (What is being done.) |

Purpose | |
         | (Why?) |
         | |

| Step | Event | Responsibility (Who?) | Description (How the task is performed.) |

(Start)

1 | (Description of task.) | _____

Reference Document # ____

2 | | _____

3 ◇ —no→ _____

yes

Ref. Test Procedure # ____

4 | | ——▶ _____

Author _____   Technical   _____
Users _____ Date ___/___/___   Management _____

Page 1 of X

Figure 5.8 Sample procedure format.

that demonstrates the employee has been trained, you will also have a record of who else can perform the job in an employee's absence. You will also notice a higher sense of ownership among the employees and a willingness to follow the procedures. Should they have a suggestion and want a change, they know where to go to get it changed.

Any changes to the procedures should require a full review by all employees and a new set of signatures. This is effective for ensuring everyone participates in the change and prevents the "no one ever told me" response. Also you will quickly reveal any objections or problems to the change prior to installing the upgrade and driving the group into a state of instability.

Keep your quality and industrial engineers in on the process to make sure that the tasks and tools are proper and also that all the appropriate safety practices are invoked.

Procedures should be stored in the areas where they are used and where they are easily accessible to the employees performing the task.

Finally, the procedures should be the property of the local supervision and management. It needs to be made clear that maintaining structural process integrity is as much a part of the job as is building the product. The direct management should be responsible for controlling how their operations run, and it is their problem if they should cause the company to fail the basic business compliance test.

11 • Establish Corrective and Preventive Action Tracking – One of the required elements of ISO 9000, Section 4.14, is the establishment of a corrective and preventive action process. Whereas the ISO 9000 series does not yet specifically state continuous improvement — and some would argue that this is the major shortfall of the standard — it does call for the establishment of a process that addresses methods used to prevent the reoccurrence of a problem and to employ an audit process that continually ensures that your operations meet the standard.

During this step, you should determine how you will respond to customer complaints, product nonconformities, and process failures to meet your defined procedures. These problems are most often caused by a failure of your process to comply with the documented procedures.

Customer complaints and internal audits usually become your most valuable indicators for the need for correction and prevention.

Foxboro developed a two pronged approach to meet these requirements. A "Customer Action Request" (CAR) process was developed to capture customer complaints and suggestions for product improvements. CARs were responded to by our service organization. A "Quality Corrective Action Request" (QCAR) process, supported by our internal audit organization, was established to address preventive process actions as described below.

Historically, when an audit team swept through the areas attempting to verify compliance to the defined system, they would find nonconformities. A nonconformity would prompt the creation of a document noting the failure with the expectation that it would be resolved within a reasonable time frame. A problem occurs when the organization only addresses the individual item identified by the audit team. For example, in the past, if an audit uncovered an untrained employee, the response from the group would have been simply to go back and train that employee. The preferred response would be to determine the root cause for the employee not being trained, and to fix the process that allowed this finding to occur.

To remedy this undesirable type of response at Foxboro, we deployed the QCAR process, as seen in Figure 5.9. The QCAR looks for the correction of the root cause of the problem, not the symptom. It requires identification of a plan with a timetable for implementation and agreement between the initiator (auditor) and the operation that the root cause of the nonconformance will be corrected. Tracking the QCAR status by your audit teams provides the second key measure for the readiness of your organization. With QCAR visibility you will gain the confidence to move ahead with the ISO 9000 certification audit by third-party certification agents.

The QCAR is the preferred method for capturing dissatisfaction throughout the company because it is a tool available to everyone for initiating a change to an unsatisfactory condition. There is one drawback to the QCAR approach: It usually takes slightly longer to make the symptom go away. But the disease is cured and the patient thrives.

#1	THE FOXBORO COMPANY	DATE	C.Q.A. 3.17.2 Page 25 QCAR #

#2	☐ INTERNAL ☐ EXTERNAL QUALITY CORRECTIVE ACTION REQUEST

#3	TO:	RETURN TO: THE FOXBORO CO ORIGINATOR'S NAME: MAIL STOP: ADDRESS

#4	CLASSIFICATION OF DEFECT	NONCONFORMANCE REPORT # _____
	☐ CRITICAL ☐ MAJOR ☐ MINOR	ORDER # _____
	REQUIRED RESPONSE (WORKING DAYS)	PART # _____ REF DOC _____
	☐ ___ DAYS ☐ 15 DAYS ☐ 30 DAYS	LOT QTY _____ REJECTED QTY _____
	☐ IMPLEMENT NEXT ORDER	SUPPLIER TYPE # _____
	PART OR ELEMENT NUMBER	

#5	PART OR ELEMENT DESCRIPTION

#6	DESCRIPTION OF DISCREPANCY (INCLUDE DATA)

#7	VERIFIED ROOT CAUSE

#8	CORRECTIVE ACTION PLAN

#9	CONTROLS TO PREVENT RECURRENCE

10	COMPLETION DATE:	IMPLEMENTED NEXT ORDER #

11	SIGNATURE	DEPT/COMPANY	DATE

12	ORIGINATOR'S VERIFICATION AND APPROVAL		
	APPROVAL YES ☐ NO ☐	VERIFIED BY :	DATE

13	REASON FOR NON APPROVAL:

Figure 5.9 Quality Corrective Action Request (QCAR) addresses the root cause of a problem, not the symptom. Tracking QCAR audit status provides an indication of readiness for an ISO 9000 audit.

12 • Train Internal Audit Teams – Internal Audit is a requirement of the standard and provides you with visibility into the status of your operations. If you are not already equipped to conduct an internal audit of your operation, we recommend sending a person to one of the many auditor training programs available that support the ISO 1011-1, 2, 3 series. It is fairly common for a group of external corporate auditors to come by once a year and take a sample survey of the level of your organization's compliance and provide you with some form of a findings listing. This is a good approach for determining major problem areas, but it does not necessarily provide the organization with the refined visibility that you will need to successfully survive an ISO 9000 audit. As an analogy, suppose you come across a mouse in your kitchen. You call in the exterminator, a couple of traps are placed, and the next day a single mouse is caught. Did the exterminator confirm that you had a mouse? Yes. Were all the mice caught? Probably not. Remember the saying, "If you see a mouse, you have a dozen." There is a high probability that you will discover another mouse. Bringing in an exterminator on a one-shot basis just doesn't work. It is better to have a cat that is relatively inexpensive to maintain in return for its vigilance and hunting expertise. At Foxboro, a corporate team goes around annually and gives us a picture of the types of problems we might have. In addition, we also created a family of "cats," referred to as internal "mini-audit teams," as seen in Figure 5.10.

The primary purpose of the internal mini-audit team is to promote the self-auditing of an organization and to provide the visibility that an external organization lacks. We started with the premise that the employees who were involved in the work were most likely to know what was really happening in their own organizations and the ideal candidates to be on the internal mini-audit teams. We selected members from different parts of the organization and trained them on the requirements of ISO 9000 and how to conduct an audit. This training was actually developed and piloted in one of our plants, and then all the operations went through the training. An agenda of the program is provided in Figure 5.11. One formally trained auditor can certainly develop a course that will produce some very effective auditors.

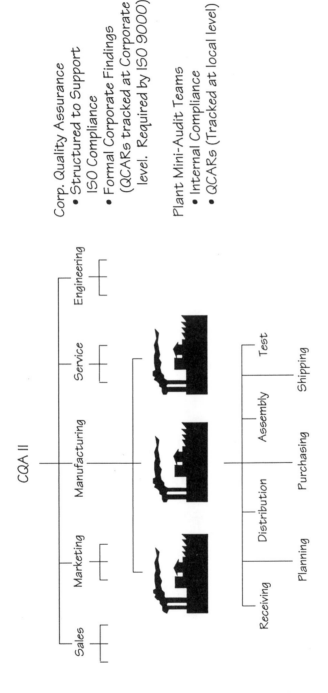

Figure 5.10 Mini-audit teams were used to promote the self-auditing of each organization and ensure readiness for the ISO 9000 audit.

PLANT AUDITOR TRAINING COURSE

THE FOXBORO COMPANY

PURPOSE

To train audit assist team members in the conduct required to be involved with customer audits of The Foxboro Company and to perform internal quality audits of a particular plant's operations within the manufacturing division.

AGENDA

1   Become familiar with ISO 9001, 10CFR50, QCAR system, and audit checklist

2   Preaudit preparation

3   Preaudit interview

4   The audit

5   Postaudit conference

6   Final report

7   Follow-up, if required

8   Review of a previous customer audit of Foxboro

9   Perform a sample audit in a random area

10 Some do and don't rules

11 Findings vs. observations

LIMIT   Eight one-hour sessions

Figure 5.11 Plant auditor training course agenda.

At Foxboro, each operation established an internal mini-audit team that systematically went through the respective organizations and conducted a thorough audit. In a typical plant, this team consisted of a buyer, a planner, an assembler, a warehouseman, and a certified lead auditor who was "home grown" and met American Society for Quality Control (ASQC) guidelines to form a complete plant mini-audit team. This team developed an aggressive schedule and went about auditing the organization. However, before the teams were sent out to do audits and generate QCARs, we recognized that we would need to change the mind-set of our management.

In the past, our management had developed an adverse sensitivity to audits and especially to findings. Yet we needed management to look at the findings (QCARs) in a very positive manner, for we intended this approach to work within their organizations.

We first convinced our senior managers that a QCAR issuance was in fact a positive event, and fortunately they had a positive response. They realized that as they were pushing their organization to move ahead quickly with scarce resources, some things would fall through the cracks. It's similar to a good basketball player — the better ones get four fouls in a game because they are playing aggressively while the ones who don't get any fouls either aren't being aggressive or they are on the bench. The senior managers took this position and reinforced it with their management teams.

This approach with the mini-audit teams had some very positive effects on the organization:

- Self-audit reduces the amount of anxiety within the operation. It had management support and was looked on as a method for improvement by the supervisors and employees.
- Having the existing staff perform the audits on a part-time basis reduced the need to fund additional staff.
- The employees looked upon this training as an opportunity for growth, as well as a return of control over their environment.
- The mini-audit teams were able to review the operations with their peers in a nondefensive manner, yielding a higher level of cooperation.

- This same audit team can also support a supplier survey program, applying ISO 9000 standards to suppliers. This also answered a common claim by suppliers that we might be holding them to a higher standard than our own organization. Your employees will also enjoy the opportunity to travel to a supplier's site, as it can generate some great ideas.

- There is also a unique phenomenon that is worthy of discussion. When the ISO 9000 registered auditors descend on your operations, you need to realize that they speak "ISOese" and probably don't understand your company terminology, nor do they understand your operations and systems. Each company "speaks" with a lot of home grown terms and acronyms. The ISO auditors will be asking questions in "ISOese" and the members of the mini-audit teams can be excellent translators. This is critical for ensuring that the proper messages are being communicated and reducing the actual stress among the groups, auditors, and the company. Mini-auditors can also help your employees feel more comfortable when approached by an auditor and can sometimes translate the questions into words the employee can understand. The mini-audit teams ensure that the auditors are being guided to the correct locations and that the responses fit the questions. Should an auditor receive an answer that seems incorrect, the issue can be dealt with before it escalates to a finding or observation. The mini-audit team member can also ensure that the auditors are receiving their answers quickly, as there is nothing more frustrating to an auditor than waiting for answers. During the audit at Foxboro, there were always two "audit assist members" from our audit teams with each ISO 9000 auditor. It was common for an ISO 9000 auditor to ask a question that would require one of the audit assist members to chase someone or something down, while the other remained to answer questions or escort the auditor. Most companies insist that visitors be escorted, and this includes auditors. You have an obligation to see they are not injured and that they are always taken to the correct locations.

• As stated earlier, mini-audit teams can provide tremendous visibility in assessing your readiness as well as projecting when you will be able to sustain a successful audit. In Foxboro's case, we tracked the number of QCARs generated by the mini-audit teams in the areas that indicated they were prepared for an audit. As noted, we considered the issuance of a QCAR as a positive indicator, and the retirement of a QCAR as another positive measure. We looked at open QCARs, those that had not yet been fixed, as less desirable, but also recognized that fixing a root cause of a problem often took time. Therefore, outstanding QCARs were considered more as an outstanding work load to be completed than as a problem. There was no pressure unless the organization had missed its own committed completion date. These measures were reported even to the president, who of course cheered on the management to generate QCARs.

More than 450 QCARs were initiated in the areas that claimed they were prepared for the audit (see Figure 5.12). The ISO 9000 audit occurred during February 1991, and we still had not closed all our QCARs. However, we did make sure they were minor and their fix status well documented. The ISO 9000 auditors, not surprisingly, found more on their own.

The deployment of the mini-audit teams in May 1990 with an aggressive schedule allowed us to determine our status by October 1990. We believed we would be ready in January of 1991, and thus arranged for a February 1991 audit. Establish an audit date that is reasonable, and hold to it. You will be amazed at how much you can accomplish when you and the organization can see them coming.

13 • Use Corporate Audit Team to Verify Compliance – The final step prior to the audit is to ensure that all the mini-audit teams have been effective. This can be determined by a Corporate Quality Assurance audit team, which not only must meet an annual audit requirement as typically defined in your own quality manual, but can use this as a vehicle

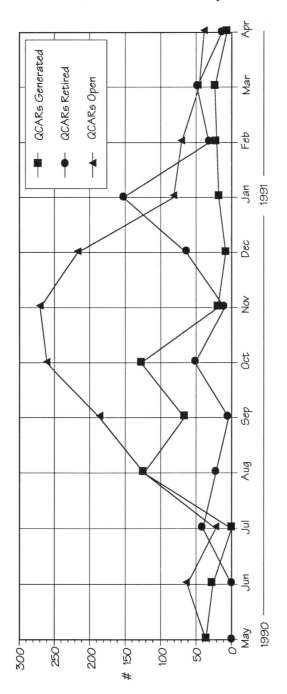

*Figure 5.12 QCARs were instrumental in preparing for the ISO 9000 audit.
Efforts focused on retiring open QCARs prior to the audit.*

for closing some remaining open findings. This team is highly visible and standalone. This group sweeps behind the plant mini-audit teams to verify that the teams are finding all the issues and that they are being corrected. Using the mini-audit teams and the corporate audit teams ensures a high degree of visibility and confidence. When the auditors first arrive, they may visit the corporate audit teams first and review the audits of the past year. This corporate-level group will meet the minimum requirement for ISO 9000. Again, the visibility of mini-audit teams is up to you. To push this "invisible mini-audit team" point a bit further, you may consider making the mini-audit teams exist only in an optional policy position format versus something required in your manual.

14 • Certification Audit – Now the fun begins. Your sales force has probably already promised the world that you will have certification and will most likely blame you for every order they lose until you become certified. The financial people have planned all those promised cost savings into next year's budget and now your president's career is tied in. You have continually reminded everyone that they don't want to be the ones that cause the company to fail — and you realize that goes for you too!

Where can it go wrong? The chart in Figure 5.13 supplied by the certification agents, Det Norske Veritas (DNV), provides some insight. DNV believes the root causes for findings are usually based on the following:

• Lack of understanding of the standard
• Lack of management commitment
• Lack of resources
• Customs of the trades

The certifying audit is extremely rigorous and comprehensive. Every site that was visited by DNV at Foxboro confirmed that "they don't miss anything, but they are fair."

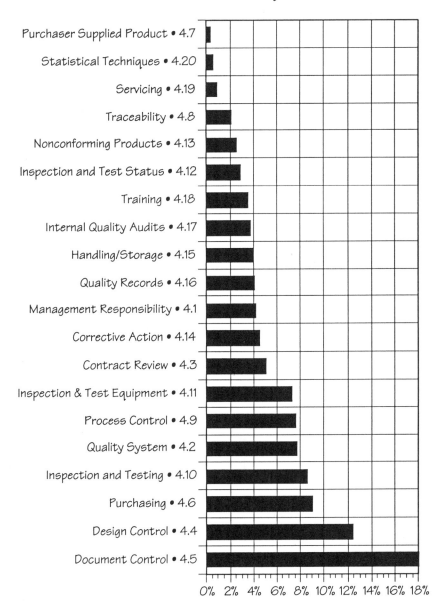

Figure 5.13 Percentage of system deficiencies registered against the requirements of ISO 9001. Source: Det Norske Veritas.

In Foxboro's case, three auditors were on-site for three weeks going through three major manufacturing facilities and one very large design and administration complex. Generally, it would take three auditors four days to complete an audit of a facility and its associated support structure within the design and administration complexes. For an idea of the on-site audit time for your operation, refer to the European Committee for Accreditation of Certified Bodies guidelines in Figure 5.14.

A dedicated office area should be set aside for the auditors' use during their stay, and it should include copies of all the relevant documents they will require to get started. Copies of our corporate manual and each operation's corporate-level manual were kept there as well.

Treat the auditors as welcome guests, not as hostile, adversarial forces. Put yourself in their place: They are often away from home facing the discomforts of business travel like hotels, airports, long car rides, late planes, and rarely a good sound sleep. Usually, their interactions with people on the job are somewhat strained, given the nature of their work, and, when the job is done, they have a mountain of paperwork to do.

Number of Employees	Initial Assessment (Man/Days) Visits			Subsequent 6 Month Audit (Man/Days)	Reassessment Visit (Man/Days)
	9001	9002	9003		
1 to 30	4	3.5	2.5	1.5	3
30 - 100	7	5.5	4	2	4
100 - 250	8	6.5	5	2.5	5
250 - 500	10	8	6	3	6
500 - 1,000	12	10	7	4	8
1,000 - 2,000	15	12	9	5	10
2,000 - 4,000	18	14.5	11	6	12
4,000 - 8,000	21	17	12.5	7	14

Figure 5.14 European Committee for Accreditation of Certified Bodies guidelines for ISO 9000 audit duration.

This description might apply to many of us, in which case, you will understand all the more the importance of a gracious reception. See that they get good rooms on the quiet side of the hotel. If there is a suite, consider the expense as an investment toward having a more rested auditor visiting your site. A little consideration in these areas will be appreciated, especially if you are attempting to demonstrate and prove a critical position with an exhausted auditor. Attention to these details will add continuity to your self-portrayal as a company focused on quality at all times and all levels.

Prior to the auditor's arrival, ensure that all the ISO 9000 Steering Council members know their roles and are ready to act as escorts between areas, along with your mini-auditors, if appropriate.

The Steering Council should consider meeting daily during the audit to review the previous day's results and implement plans to correct any findings prior to the conclusion of the audit. Depending on the type of agency you are using, it may be possible to correct a minor finding prior to the certification agent leaving the premises and thereby assist your meeting the minimum requirement or reduce the follow-up audit duration. It will also improve your score for those who operate under a scoring system.

Once the auditors are on site, bring them to your conference room and begin the orientation to the manuals as well as to the various safety and escort requirements. As stated earlier, promote a very open and friendly atmosphere. The auditors should have been selected with the understanding that they want you to succeed. On the other hand, they have their reputation to protect and the possibility of losing their certification is very real. Their job is to ensure that you have:

• Established a quality policy
• Developed an appropriate quality system
• Documented the system as required
• Effectively implemented the system
• Met the requirements of the ISO 9000 standard

A typical audit proceeds in this manner: You greet the auditors, do the orientation, and assign team members. The lead auditor then takes control of the audit, and from then on the approach is at the discretion of this individual. The first stop might be a visit to your formal internal audit group where the auditors will ask to see the last year's internal audits. They want to confirm that you are actually conducting audits and will want to see schedules and activities associated with the audits, such as follow-ups to previous findings. They are also looking for trends, areas where your own audit teams repeatedly find problems. They will take their cues from the findings of these audits and look in the same areas. Finally, they are looking for open findings that are critical to the standard. If your own audit organization has left an open critical finding, it is an immediate "gotcha." If it is critical, the auditors will simply go to the area identified, confirm the shortfall, and thank you for inviting them as they head home. It is absolutely critical that all open corporate findings are closed.

After the auditors are firmly convinced that you have an aggressive audit program, they might make one more stop, prior to moving ahead with the audit in earnest. This next stop provided us with visible proof of the thoroughness of their audit and should also help you realize, as one of our employees so aptly stated, "you can't hide anything." They might visit your local accounting organization to gain access to all your departmental account codes, thereby ensuring access to all the desired areas and organizations. If you were thinking about making an organization disappear, or a tool room vanish, think again. Their methodology involved going to central information points first, then looking for abnormalities, and then making sure their audit plan incorporated an investigation of these abnormalities.

A typical example was that of Foxboro's calibration control. The audit team asked to see how calibration and the maintenance records were controlled. While they were verifying that the system existed, they also reviewed the records to see who had not returned tools. These locations then became the primary focus for investigation. With the team now armed with account codes and a year's worth of internal audit data they begin the process of investigation. This process usually follows the flow of the product, to your level of intended certification. In the case of ISO 9001, this means all the way back to your sales office.

You can expect that they will visit a local sales branch (if it is in your factory, that will be the logical target). They will ask where the orders come in, pick one up, and then say, "show me." The show me involves asking the employees how they handle the orders, how the orders are entered, and what do they do when they have a problem. The auditors may ask you to show them some training records (for both inside and outside employees; even the sales people if appropriate) and possibly ask questions like, "Do you have a quality policy? What is it?"

After the employees have come to grips with their nervousness, they point to the wall and say, "that's it" or mumble something about customer satisfaction and they begin answering the questions, and showing the necessary documents. When the auditors are satisfied, they will migrate down through your order scheduling department to again ask similar questions, with the focus on verifying that you are accurately processing the order and accurately quoting deliveries and handling the exceptions.

Finally, your order makes it to the production areas, and there the audit team will seem to split. The majority of the auditors' time, as much as 80%, will be spent in the manufacturing process. The rest of the audit team migrates up through engineering, design, and marketing.

As the audit team goes through engineering and design, the primary focus will be on two areas. A potential trouble spot can be the coordination of documentation between manufacturing and engineering. They will want to see not only that the proper documents are sent to manufacturing, but also that some form of acknowledgment is sent back to the originator ensuring that manufacturing has actually seen the documents. The other area is in the design review and sign off. The auditors will be looking to see a process that assures all the appropriate work has been completed to assure the product meets both the performance and safety requirements that it claims to support. They want a signature to verify that what has been designed is what marketing asked for and is what is being communicated to manufacturing.

The audit team will eventually migrate up to the marketing organization and verify the communication process between engineering and marketing. They will also look to ensure that what marketing is selling is in fact what engineering is being asked to design.

Meanwhile, the audit team on the assembly floor is interacting with your plant people. They will spend most of their time on the manufacturing floor and will generally avoid the supervision. They will walk into an area, introduce themselves, and ask what the employee does. After the employee describes his or her tasks to the auditors and it is relevant to the auditors' area of inquiry, the employee can expect additional questions such as:

• Do you have a quality policy here?

• Tell me about this machine; how do you operate it?

• Where are the procedures you consult if you have any questions? (The employee must be able to have easy access and personally show the auditors.)

• Were you trained before you started working alone, and could you get that record for me?

• How do you know when you are making the product correctly? Can you tell when it is good or bad? Show me. (Make sure there is some documented method for differentiation and that it was included as part of the training record.)

• If you have a problem with the machine or material coming out, what do you do? (You will need a documented process outlined on how you control nonconforming materials.)

• How do you know those tools you are using are acceptable? Which ones need to be calibrated, and how do you know when to send them back?

• I noticed that you are using control charts. What do you do when they go out of control — like right there on the chart — what happened and what did you do? Could you show me the procedure and your training record on how you were trained on these charts? (Make sure your employees who are marking the charts are keeping records on those out-of-control events; the auditors are looking for some form of documented proof that the employee did take some action versus ignoring the event. Also ensure your charts are maintained in an on-line dynamic fashion. Charts updated after the product has left the area are in jeopardy of being considered ineffective to your preventative program.)

• How do you know you are building the right thing? Could you show me the assembly documents or model?

After the auditors have completed their questions they will apply a score or make a binary decision based upon the approach, the documentation, and the execution. The auditors will also look for documentation, old and current. Ensure that you have all your old documents (or models) removed or clearly marked, for example, "not for manufacturing use." They will be calling their fellow auditors who are visiting engineering and confirming revisions and dates. They will be looking at your test equipment to ensure not only that the equipment is under some form of calibration control, but also that the test requirements and outputs are those specified by engineering. They will look to see that your manufacturing operations have procedures for the update of these documents.

The auditors will progress through the operation to final testing, then to packaging, and on to shipping. They will also go into your service operations and will treat them as they would any manufacturing operation.

After finishing in the marketing and engineering areas, they will then descend upon your materials organization. They will review your planning operations — make sure you have a procedure on how you set master schedules. They will then focus on your purchasing, quality, and engineering interface. Your purchasing employees must be well versed in your supplier procurement process and the methods used to survey your suppliers and the materials being brought into your operation and the communications of changes with the supplier. After they are satisfied they will head out to your material handling areas. Ensure that your employees know their procedures and materials. For example, if you call for handling with Electro Static Discharge (ESD) bags, the employees need to be able to differentiate them from regular plastic bags and to be wearing a discharge device when they handle the materials. If a material is considered defective, ensure that it is maintained in a separate flow, and that all employees can recognize it as nonconforming material.

Upon completion of the materials areas the auditors will go to Incoming Inspection, looking for continuity between engineering and purchasing, as well as the usual competence and records.

After they have sufficiently covered all of the key points they will confer among themselves. You will probably already know the verdict, but they will officially tell you at the exit interview. If you pass, congratulations for achieving certification on the first audit. It is a major accomplishment.

If you fail the first time, you are in good company. According to a study reported in the July 1993 edition of *Quality Progress*, 60% of companies fail in their first attempt at ISO 9000 registration. Your challenge will be to salvage as much of the positive audit as possible and arrange with the auditors for a revisit, quickly. Each certification agent has his or her own approach, and it is best to clarify this early on and press the agents to live up to their earlier promises. If the audit goes badly initially, don't let them stop there — keep them going for two reasons. First, you need the visibility, and, second, your organization needs the exposure. You will pay more, but it will be worth it. If you will recall, you thought you were ready before the audit and without the auditors' visibility and their exposure to your management it is most likely you will have another bad experience, unless something changes. After two bad experiences you could be putting your career in jeopardy, as management will usually opt for a new team and coach.

Hopefully, you will have a positive audit and hold a celebration to congratulate the entire company as you all will have earned it. Eventually the certificate comes in and all is forgiven, but hopefully not forgotten. There is still the distinct possibility that when the auditors come back to close out some questionable findings, you could stumble, even though you had passed the first time. The other point is to realize that they will be back every six months (some auditors only every 12 months) to perform another shorter but more rigorous and in-depth audit focused on a specific operation. Passing these regular audits ensures continued ISO 9000 certification and causes you to get even better.

Also, remember, if one of your customers lodges a complaint against your operations, the auditor is likely to investigate the complaint at the next audit, or, if the complaint is serious enough, you may be required to move up the regularly scheduled audit.

6

What Do They Really Mean?

At times you will read the standard and say, "what does it really mean?" This chapter will go through the elements of the ISO 9000 standard as an auditor might. It will rephrase the ISO 9001 standard elements by section, clarifying and augmenting each area and addressing the questions that would likely arise in reading the sections.

4.1 Management Responsibility

Deming, Juran, and other quality experts believed that management was primarily responsible for 80% to 90% of an organization's problems. Appropriately, management responsibility is the first element of the ISO 9000 standard.

4.1.1 Quality policy – Management must define and document its quality policy to ensure commitment to quality and to the minimum requirements of ISO 9000. Management must see that this policy is understood and implemented throughout the organization.

4.1.2 Organization – This subsection requires you to be able to prove that the template for your organization's quality approach is effective and defines responsibility. The standard calls for you to address problems systematically and solve them by attacking the root causes.

4.1.2.1 Responsibility and authority – An authority must be identified who can manage and verify that work affecting quality is performed as documented by your quality system. This person must have the freedom and authority to ensure the organization addresses and prevents nonconforming activities, maintains records of quality problems, and causes the organization to correct the nonconformities. This individual will later investigate and verify that the solution has succeeded. He or she must also be able to stop the operation or a shipment if required and report it appropriately. Most companies provide an organization chart, with a path from the president down through the line personnel, with designated individuals having specific responsibilities for Quality Control or Quality Assurance.

4.1.2.2 Resources – Management must maintain an in-house verification capacity for the primary purpose of conducting an internal audit. Audit personnel must be adequately trained for verification activities (see 4.17, Internal Audits and 4.18, Training).

Internal auditors will be required to verify that your entire operation conforms to your quality plan, as well as to all the elements of ISO 9000. These audits need to be carried out on a regular basis (at least once per year) to ensure compliance. "Regular" means that your organization should be prepared to be audited by a third party at any given time with a high probability of passing.

The dynamics of your process and common industry practice will dictate the interval of your audits. Audits as described in this section must be carried out by a trained, independent party that is not immediately responsible for the area being audited.

These audits need to carry the appropriate level of documentation. You must prove to the third-party auditors that they were carried out as part of an overall comprehensive plan for the audit of the organization and that they are rigorous in nature (i.e., you will be required to show comment and actions).

4.1.2.3 Management representative – A senior management representative must be designated to ensure that the requirements of ISO 9000 and all other defined quality standards are established and maintained.

People who are designated as the quality contacts can have multiple functions within your organization; therefore, it is not necessary that they have a strictly quality-related title. However, you need to be careful of the fox-in-the-hen-house syndrome. It is quite possible that your senior production manager within the manufacturing organization is responsible for total quality in his organization, including the verification and inspection aspects. If so, there needs to be a very strong case made, supported by documented evidence, that this individual is acting impartially and meeting the full intent of the standard. An easy way to define the quality responsibility is to designate quality responsibilities from the president to the assembly-line person on your corporate organization chart.

4.1.3 Management review – The management of your organization must regularly review the results of the quality system to determine that it is doing the intended job. This review should be based on measures that include the internal audit data and customer feedback, as well as appropriate incremental quality improvement data indicating the overall effectiveness of your system. You will need to document this review. These reviews should occur regularly or when an indicator reveals an undesirable result. If you have an active quality council, continually upgrading your operations, recordings of these meeting, and upgrades will effectively serve this requirement.

4.2 Quality System

4.2.1 General – The intention of this element is to ensure that you define, document, and maintain your quality system in a way that results in satisfaction of your customer's expectations. This means that you must have a manual that incorporates the ISO 9000 standard. This manual must also be able to reference the procedures that you are using to meet the standard. Additional information on this can be found in Appendix 2 of this book and in the ISO 10013 (guidance on quality manuals) document.

4.2.2 Quality system procedures – You must prepare documented and controlled procedures that meet the ISO 9000 and any other relevant requirements. For example, if you are telling your customers that you are meeting G.M.P. or Military standards, then your procedures and manual should reflect it.

It goes without saying that your actual practices should meet your defined procedures. But, how much do you have to document? There is no easy answer; it is a balance between the dependence of the task on quality and the complexity and the level of recorded training that you have provided beforehand. An excellent training program can significantly reduce your procedural load.

4.2.3 Quality Planning – The establishment of a documented quality plan is a required element. The good news is that it can look any way that you want it to look, and in most cases all you really need to do is reference your procedures that you have in place. You might also consider going a step further and define your quality plan via a relationship diagram — groups of boxes (functions) that connect to other boxes, with descriptions of the relationship. This diagram should reference where your quality plans come from, where your in-process controls are established, inspection equipment is defined, where production resources and training are determined, where design review is developed as well as the test procedures, who establishes the quality control techniques, points of inspection, measures required for process capabilities, test and verification. The plan needs to address who will be responsible for the clarification of the standards for acceptance as well as how records are generated, their contents, and how they must be kept.

4.3 Contract Review

4.3.1 General – Your organization must have a systematic and documented method for ensuring that you understand and can meet your customers' needs. If your specifications differ from your customer requirements, there must be an orderly method for reconciliation. Finally, you must have a way to ensure that you have adequate capacity to meet the combined needs of all customers, if applicable. The ISO

9000 standard also suggests that ongoing communications be maintained with the customer during the life of the order as appropriate.

4.3.2 Review – You are required to review your customers' orders prior to accepting them. To be considered effective, you must first ensure a complete understanding of what they are asking for. The standard indicates a preference for a written order, but the authors understand that a verbal order is fairly common. In this case, they ask you to put a methodology in place that ensures the verbal order is confirmed and agreed to at the time of acceptance. When you receive the order, you must make sure you can honor it in all respects.

4.3.3 Amendment to contract – On occasion your customer may change their order, or worse yet, you may not be able to meet your original commitment. You must have a documented system in place that defines how you go about communicating and executing these changes with both your customer, as well as your own internal organization.

4.3.4 Records – Upon review of a customer order by an authorized person, a record of the order and the review must be maintained.

4.4 Design Control

4.4.1 General – This section requires you to maintain a documented process for the design of your product that produces the performance characteristics you promise your customers.

4.4.2 Design and development planning – This design plan must define how the design process will be carried out. It encompasses all levels of staff involved, their communications, and process paths. The design process must undergo regular and documented management reviews. Those in charge of design control must staff the function with appropriately trained people and equipment.

4.4.3 Organizational and technical interfaces – All interfaces between the design and other organizations required to design a product need to be identified, communicated, and reviewed regularly. For example, marketing, sales, manufacturing, legal, and product safety. The information required for the design process from other organizations (input requirements) must also be defined.

4.4.4 Design input – You must have a defined system to ensure all appropriate design requirements are received by the design group. This includes all customer regulatory requirements. A listing of specifications and unique characteristics of the product must be maintained. The design group must actively communicate, detail, and resolve inconsistencies in the product requirements.

4.4.5 Design review – You will need to perform design reviews at defined stages of product development. You need to define what is involved at each stage, and who needs to be involved at that particular stage. This means that at some point during the design, you must invite all those you have identified to approve of the design (4.4.3). Their acceptance must be recorded and maintained.

4.4.6 Design output – The output of the design process will include documented drawings, test requirements and tolerance requirements, materials specifications, appropriate assembly instructions, and test methodologies. Design output is to be documented and expressed in terms of requirements, calculations, and analyses. This output will also specifically reference all the appropriate regulatory or association standards and any critical requirements to the design that relate to the safe assembly and operation of the product.

4.4.7 Design verification – You will conduct a formal and documented review of the product design to ensure that all defined criteria are satisfied. This design review should include qualification testing, comparison with a similar design or any other calculation that will enable you to ensure that you meet the design input requirements. These verification measures will be recorded and retained along with the design verification acceptance.

4.4.8 Design validation – You need to ensure the final product meets the design input, which should be the same as the customer's requirements. This validation should occur in the same environment for which the product is intended. If you have multiple environments and intended uses, it should be tested for all of them. The product must meet the full requirements.

4.4.9 Design changes – The process for making changes to your design should be documented. The routine should essentially meet the same criteria as those for a new design with all the authorized signatures.

4.5 Document and Data Control

4.5.1 General – All documents that are pertinent to the ISO 9000 standard must be under some type of formal documentation control, with procedures defining their establishment, review, upgrade, authorization, and removal upon obsolescence.

This includes external reference documents used in areas such as design and testing. The documents can be in any media you choose, but they must be easily obtainable and usable.

4.5.2 Documentation approval and issue – All your documents and data will require approval by an authorized person. This means that you must formally authorize individuals and they must be capable of assessing the adequacy of the document. You will then have to maintain a master listing of all the documents being used and their appropriate revision status. This listing is required to ensure that only current revision documents are being used and that all obsolete documents are removed. The current documents must be available at their point of use and if for some reason you require that the old documents be available, they must be properly identified as not intended for current use.

4.5.3 Document changes – Any changes made to the documentation will require the same review and authorization that the establishment of the original document requires. When possible, an overview of the change to the document should be included with the new release. It is recommended that the changes to prior documents be noted to assist those working with the document.

4.6 Purchasing

4.6.1 General—You are required to conduct your purchasing operations in a systematic fashion that ensures you are obtaining the proper materials for the organization's specified requirements.

4.6.2 Evaluation of sub-contractors – Assessment of a supplier must include a formal documented review methodology. The organization must maintain the assessment records of a supplier and a formal documented listing of suppliers who meet this approved process. This approved supplier listing must be available to those using it.

The supplier evaluation process used to determine acceptability is based on the type of product being secured, past experience with the supplier, and its capabilities. In all cases, the assessment must specify the quality of the materials received. You must maintain records of the supplier's evaluation as well as the acceptability of the materials received. A somewhat misunderstood fact is that your suppliers do not have to be certified to ISO 9000. They only have to provide you with good materials that meet your requirements on time.

4.6.3 Purchasing data – The material being purchased must be fully described. This includes specific part identification. You will also describe process requirements, inspection instructions, special markings, and any other detailed information relevant to the acceptance of the material.

The purchase document must include notation of compliance to any relevant standard (ISO 9000 may be one of those standards). Prior to the release of the specification requirement to the supplier, an appropriately trained individual must review it to ensure adequacy. This individual can be the originator of the requirement.

4.6.4 Verification of purchased product – It is the purchaser's option to perform a source inspection of the product or to perform the inspection on the purchaser's site. In either case, inspection location does not absolve the supplier of the responsibility to inspect and fully comply with its own quality policy, as described to the purchaser. If the purchaser provides for source inspection at the supplier's site, the purchaser does not surrender the right to reject the material at any later time. If you decide to perform a source inspection, it must be noted on your purchase order to the supplier.

4.7 Control of Customer Supplied Product

You must establish procedures for the inspection, storage, handling, and maintenance of materials provided to you by your customer for eventual incorporation into a supplied product. Should this material become unusable for any reason, it must be segregated, identified, and reported to your customer.

This could be considered a "mirror" policy of your expectations and policies for the proper handling of your own materials. Your supplier's unique expectations will be defined in the initial contract, and procedures will be required to support such activities.

4.8 Product Identification and Traceability

You must maintain procedures for the proper identification and documentation of materials as they move through the production, installation, and delivery processes to ensure that the customer's requirements are satisfied.

Second, depending on your customer's requirements, you may need to address production lot identification or component traceability. The standard says this is to be done "where appropriate," meaning as required by your customer. Your customer may request that your product have varying degrees of traceability. Your must ensure there are formal and documented methods and records in place to satisfy this request .

4.9 Process Control

Process control refers to the entire process of producing a product and the method by which you control and ensure that your processes are followed — it is not limited to some form of statistical process control. The standard frequently uses the term "procedures" when referring to process control.

You must provide a controlled work environment that ensures that the quality of the product is adequate and in conformance with the documentation and record requirements of ISO 9000. This requires you to provide adequate and controlled written instructions or representative samples that ensure proper assembly and workmanship standards. These standards should define the criteria for acceptable workmanship.

The process should define the equipment, environment, reference standards, and quality plans, and must include regular monitoring during production. The equipment used by the employees must have appropriate operating instructions and maintenance plans.

Work instructions must be reviewed by authorized personnel. These instructions are required whenever their absence could adversely affect the quality of the output. The instructions should be reviewed periodically to ensure adequacy and proper alignment with other procedures. The work instructions must clearly define the acceptance criteria so the operator can differentiate the good from the bad.

A "special process" is any process that cannot be fully confirmed through immediate testing or inspection so a defect may only surface when the product is being used by the customer. Typical examples are welding, paint applications (Zyglow inspection), and heat treatment of materials. These processes require identification as special processes, clearly defined process parameters, operation by appropriately trained personnel using qualified equipment, and continuous monitoring with supporting records. Special processes must also meet the full requirements of this section.

4.10 Inspection and Testing

4.10.1 General – This element deals with the testing of your materials as they move through your process as well as the final inspection of the product. The testing operations must be carried out in accordance with your documented procedures and supported with records that indicate the status of the material and eventual satisfactory status of all requirements prior to the product's release.

This element also deals with emergency situations that occur in real life. For example, the standard allows you to release incoming materials for urgent production without inspection. However, if you to bypass inspection, you must employ a "positive recall procedure." This procedure requires that you track this material and be able to identify it, should further testing indicate that your materials or workmanship are unsatisfactory.

4.10.2 Receiving inspection and testing – No material should be incorporated into the product without verification to the product specifications. This does not mean all your material must undergo a full specification inspection. "Partials" are legitimate as long as they meet your inspection plans. If, due to emergency, the incoming material is used without verification, it will require designated authorization, full documentation, and tracking (positive recall procedure). All preverified materials should be maintained in a segregated area according to a documented process.

The verification of the incoming product must conform to your quality plan and documented procedures. Verification can take many acceptable forms and is not necessarily delegated to the receiving inspection organization, however, records must be maintained to meet the defined inspection requirements specified in your procedures. When establishing inspection schemes you should consider recorded evidence of receipt histories as well as the process capability of the supplier.

4.10.3 In-process inspection and testing – You must document your in-process inspection procedures and test points and carry out the defined inspections. The level of in-process inspection is determined by your own operations, and, with the exception of special process inspections, there is no additional requirement.

If in-process inspection is required, you will need to provide holding points for nonconforming materials. The ISO 9000 standard encourages the use of in-process inspection as a method for minimizing defects and allows in-process inspections to act as part of the final inspection and test if appropriate.

4.10.4 Final inspection and testing – You are required to perform a full inspection and test of your final product as specified in your quality plan and documented procedures. This full inspection and test must verify that the inspection data fully meet the specifications of the product, as defined by your quality plan. Final inspection should incorporate the results of previous inspections and their successful satisfaction of requirements. You are required to hold the product and defer its shipment or release until all inspections have been completed and the product has met all the specifications. Your inspection record should indicate who authorized the release of the product (of course, this person must be authorized to do so).

4.10.5 Inspection and test records – You must keep records to demonstrate that your product has met the testing requirements and that all the tests were conducted per your quality plan (also see section 4.16).

4.11 Control of Inspection, Measuring, and Test Equipment

4.11.1 General –You must ensure the proper maintenance, review, and control of *all* of your final test, calibration, and any other test equipment (including jigs, fixtures, templates, patterns, and software) as defined by your quality plan. This equipment must be capable of measuring to the level of accuracy specified in the test requirements. Your employees must have been training in the use and proper applications of the equipment. If your customers request the technical test data on your inspection equipment to conduct their own study to determine functional adequacy, they must be made available to them.

4.11.2 Control procedure –To comply with this section of the standard, you should:
a. Identify what measure is to be made, by what piece of equipment, and to what specific tolerances.
b. Identify and calibrate all test equipment at regular intervals of time or usage. The equipment must be capable of making the required measurements. The calibration of this equipment must be compared with a known "good" with a clear path to a nationally recognized standard.   Calibration cycle times are usually based on the manufacturer's guidelines, or less often by history and usage. If there are no standards to reference, you must document how to meet your desired standard.
c. Have a calibration system to identify the equipment to be used, where it is used, the method for confirmation, the frequency of inspection, and the procedure for when it is out of conformance.
d. Place some type of identification mark on the equipment to show its current calibration status.
e. Maintain records on the calibration with at least one prior record available.
f. Document the occurrence and return to the prior calibration for review should you find a device out of calibration. When a nonconformance trend is indicated, correct the nonconformance by shortening the calibration cycle or replacing a tool. Notification should also be sent to the usage point of the calibration equipment.
g. Ensure that the area is suitable for the testing and usage of the equipment.
h. Properly store and maintain (through employee training) the calibration equipment.
i. Permit only authorized personnel to make adjustments to the equipment or software.

Not all your measurement or calibration equipment is required to satisfy the previous requirements, only those used in the final product test inspections or as defined in your quality plan. If in-process inspections are used to validate requirements within the process, and they support your final inspection and testing activity, then they must be made part of your calibration control scheme. Should you determine that a particular instrument is not required to meet the ISO 9000 criteria, then you may exempt it by identifying it as such. However, keeping as many pieces of equipment as possible in compliance with these requirements will help you to produce the best product at the lowest cost and achieve the goal of zero defects. Third-party certification agents take a dim view if you try to stipulate that only your final test equipment needs calibration control. They will usually cite a failure in your corrective action process if you attempt to use this loophole. We advise that you discuss this with your auditor beforehand.

4.12 Inspection and Test Status

As products go through the various testing areas, the material and products must carry test identification relative to their status. Identification can include stamps, labels, tags, records, or diskettes. Those products that fail to meet the testing or inspection criteria should be physically separated from the rest. If separation is not possible, a very clear identifier of its unsatisfactory status must be displayed. This identification should follow the product through the entire production process. These records must indicate the authorized person who allowed the proper release of the product. These records shall conform to section 4.16, quality records requirements.

4.13 Control of Nonconforming Product

4.13.1 General – Upon identification of a nonconforming material or product, the item must be segregated, when possible, and identified as not suitable for use. All operations must have procedures in place to define the process that handles the nonconformance. When appropriate, the nonconformance must carry documentation that will support the evaluation of the product and disposition. A notification of the nonconformance and disposition shall be forwarded to all parties affected or involved in the nonconformance.

4.13.2 Nonconforming product review and disposition – The evaluation of nonconforming material must be conducted by an authorized individual as defined by your documented procedures. If the authorized individual determines that the product is acceptable as is, or requires a regrade, a return, or is to be scrapped, the accompanying document will reflect this activity and only then may you proceed to process the material. Should the authorized agent determine that rework or repair is required, the original document outlining the nonconformance must remain active until a reinspection of the material is done and only then may the issue be closed. The document prepared for the identification of the nonconforming product should include a description of the inadequacy, and a full description of the activities required for correction and disposition. If you determine that the product does not fully meet the specifications, but you still consider it acceptable from the customer's perspective, a full report of the material's condition must be made available to the customer and this condition must be recorded and retained.

4.14 Corrective and Preventive Action

4.14.1 General –You are required to take corrective and preventive actions based on any customer complaint, service failures, audits of operations, and quality records. This action must look for the root cause of the problem and put corrective procedures and practices in place that will prevent future occurrences. Your organization must put controls in place to ensure that all corrective actions are carried out, that they have been effective, and that the associated effort is commensurate with the potential risk to the customer.

4.14.2 Corrective Action – You must maintain a documented system with records that effectively collect and resolve customer complaints as well as product failures, including:

a. A documented system on how you handle, track, and resolve complaints.

b. Performing a recorded investigation related to the complaint.

c. Establishing a corrective action that will remedy the cause of the problem.

d. Fixing the cause of the problem and confirm that your fix worked.

4.14.3 Preventive action – You must have procedures in place to systematically review your operations to ensure compliance to your quality plan. To meet this requirement, you must perform the following:

a. Engage in a review of your operations with information from internal audits, quality records, service reports, and customer complaints. The intention is to use the records to eliminate the causes of these nonconformities.

b. Create a plan to eliminate these nonconformities.

c. Execute your corrective plan and ensure that it was effective in eliminating the problem.

d. Ensure that the appropriate actions taken to remedy the nonconformities have been reviewed by management. This would include not only the corrective response, but the procedures that have been upgraded in response to the nonconformity.

4.15 Handling, Storage, Packaging, Preservation, and Delivery

4.15.1 General – All activities related to the handling, storage, packaging, and delivery of the product must have fully documented and maintained procedures.

4.15.2 Handling – Your methods for handling must ensure the product remains undamaged and will not suffer from deterioration. This includes full documentation of methods and training to ensure safety of personnel and product.

4.15.3 Storage—You must have secure and segregated storage of raw and finished materials to prevent deterioration, damage, and mixing. You must also have documented methods for the transfer of the materials. Documented procedures and methods should also include the regular assessment of the stored materials to ensure material integrity. You also must, at regular intervals, review your stock materials to monitor and prevent deterioration.

4.15.4 Packaging – The operation must maintain formal and documented packaging procedures, marking requirements, and instructions. The packaging instructions must be documented, preservation methods outlined, and equipment used that will not damage the materials. Personnel must be trained in the packaging techniques and equipment used. The product should be marked in accordance with specifications.

4.15.5 Preservation – Preservation methods will be documented. The materials must remain segregated and maintained until the product has been accepted by customer or per contract agreement.

4.15.6 Delivery – Delivery of the product is made in accordance with the customer contract. Special protection should be extended to support the intact arrival if specified. The delivery methods and practices must be documented and the employees trained for this task.

4.16 Control of Quality Records

You must retain records that verify product compliance to requirements. Your records must also demonstrate the verified effectiveness of your operations through internal audits, corrective actions, senior management reviews, assessment of suppliers, calibration, training, customer contracts, design reviews, product nonconformances, inspection and testing, and product identification.

Records should be defined, filed, and maintained to allow for easy access. They should identify the process and products involved. Record retention procedures must be documented and support customer agreements. Quality records must be stored for minimum deterioration, easy retrieval, and for a reasonable period of time (e.g. warranty period). If you reference records outside of your organization, you must maintain documented procedures supporting their maintenance.

4.17 Internal Quality Audits

You must carry out a comprehensive review of your organization to verify the effectiveness of your quality system and compliance with the ISO 9000 standard. This review should take the form of scheduled audits of the various areas, based on the relative importance of the operations and activities. Audits are to be conducted in accordance with your documented procedures by trained individuals. The results of the audits must be documented and presented to management personnel for timely corrective action of any nonconformances cited, and tracked to ensure follow-through. Follow-up audits must be conducted to confirm the corrective action.

Audit frequency will be determined based on experience as well as the importance to the products being produced. Generally, no more than one year should elapse between audits of the same area to maintain compliance.

Audits are carried out according to a documented plan that will specify not only locations and time, but also the qualifications of the auditors, the output required, the method for conducting the audit, and who will receive the results. Audits shall be conducted by personnel independent of the operation being audited and trained in ISO 9000 requirements.

4.18 Training

Training must be provided and documented for all personnel whose activities affect quality. Personnel must be trained in the specific tasks assigned, qualified to perform these tasks, and supported with documentation and records of training. These records must be maintained to reflect the current task.

Your quality plan must outline the procedures for identifying the tasks that require training. Training can be based on formal education, supervised training on the job, or past experience. In any case, a formal record must be maintained and approved by an authorized individual as defined in the procedures.

If a generic job description exists, procedures should require the integration of both the job description and any additional requirements as seen in Figure 6.1. Requirements that are not included in the job description, should be added to a department specific record. Therefore, three documents should exist:

- A procedure on how to develop the training requirement.
- The generic job description.
- The specific training record that incorporates the additional requirements, references to the generic job description, with the supervisor's and employee's signatures validating the successful training.

4.19 Servicing

Based on your policies and customer contracts, you will provide service to the level defined in your quality plan. All those activities performed must comply with the ISO 9000 standard. You will develop plans, procedures, training, documentation, and testing methods to support the committed level of service. You will have a documented process that verifies that you have met all the customer requirements.

4.20 Statistical Techniques

4.20.1 Identification of need – You are required to review your process for possible applications of statistical tools. The intended purpose is to ensure that you control and verify your process capability as well as the product characteristics.

4.20.2 Procedures – You may use statistical techniques to validate the product, material, or process. These techniques must be documented and approved. Operators must be trained and demonstrate proficiency.

The ISO 9000 standard is interpretive to accommodate different types of businesses. It is important to ensure that your interpretation is shared by your auditor. Consider the rephrasing of the standard in this chapter as a supplement to other guidance documents such as ISO 9004.

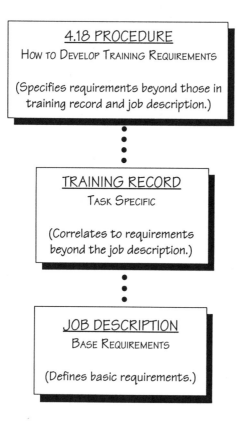

Figure 6.1 Procedures for training requirements (4.18) should build upon job descriptions and training records.

Appendix 1

Are You Ready?

The following questions will help you gauge your readiness. They are organized for specific organizations within the firm including:

- Management
- Order Processing
- Research, Design, and Development
- Planning
- Procurement
- Stores/Material Handling
- Production
- Inspection
- Shipping/Transport
- Servicing

Consider asking your major organizational groups to verify that they can answer each of the questions under their heading. These questions could also become the basis for review by your internal audit organizations. Although they are not all inclusive, be assured that if you don't ask them, the ISO 9000 auditors will.

Management

4.1 Management Responsibility
☐   Have you documented your quality policy and stated your corporate mission clearly?
☐   Is there an ISO 9000 program manager?

- ☐ Is your organization trained to understand your quality policy, and is the policy being maintained?
- ☐ Are there job descriptions that define quality authority and responsibility?
- ☐ Are trained individuals assigned to internal audit activities and are their audit reports transmitted to senior management?
- ☐ Has management reviewed all final inspection and test procedures to ensure adequacy and compliance with customer contracts?
- ☐ Is the total quality system reviewed by management regularly?
- ☐ Is there a senior management representative with the responsibility and authority to ensure effective problem resolutions according to the procedures?
- ☐ Is there a sufficient number of trained people allocated for verification?
- ☐ How does management adequately ensure ISO 9000 compliance?

4.2 Quality System
- ☐ Do you have an index of all your procedures and revisions referenced in your manual?
- ☐ Do you have a Quality Plan referenced in your manual?
- ☐ Do you have an ISO 9000 manual reviewed by senior management?

4.3 Contract Review
- ☐ Does management review your ability to meet contractual commitments?

4.4 Design Control
- ☐ Are design activities formalized and cohesive?

4.5 Document and Data Control
- ☐ Is the documentation system reviewed and approved by management?

☐ Do your documentation control procedures ensure the acquisition and control of all external documents, such as reference design and test standards?

4.13 Control of Nonconforming Product
☐ Is disposition authority defined?

4.14 Corrective and Preventive Action
☐ Has management reviewed the process for corrective action and verified that all requirements are met?
☐ How has management demonstrated involvement in the corrective action process?
☐ Is someone in your organization determining the priorities for addressing corrective actions?

4.16 Control of Quality Records
☐ Do you have records of management review of the quality system?

4.17 Internal Quality Audits
☐ Do you have records of management review of internal audits, schedules, and results?

4.18 Training
☐ Has management ensured that the training program requirements have been documented and implemented for all employees that have an effect on quality?

Order Processing

4.1 Management Responsibility
☐ Has responsibility for contract review been defined?
☐ Have contract review activities been defined?

4.3 Contract Review

☐ Are there procedures established to support customer inquiries?

☐ Are order preparation and review procedures established to ensure that customer requirements can be met?

☐ Are methods established for clarifying customer orders when they are incomplete or unclear?

☐ How do you verify proper translation of customer orders into internal work orders?

☐ Are communications to customers clearly defined and formalized?

4.5 Document and Data Control

☐ Are there clear procedures for the creation of internal work orders based on customer contracts?

☐ Are customer change order procedures documented and properly processed?

☐ Are methods in place to communicate changes in product status to customers with existing contracts?

4.13 Control of Nonconforming Product

☐ Are customer complaints documented and supported by written procedures and their disposition monitored and recorded?

4.14 Corrective and Preventive Action

☐ Is there an effective corrective action process employed to eliminate ongoing customer complaints, and is it reviewed to ensure root cause problems are remedied?

4.16 Control of Quality Records

☐ Are records of customer contracts properly maintained for the required period?

☐ Are customer complaints recorded and maintained for analysis?

4.17 Internal Quality Audits
☐ Have corrective actions been initiated based on deficiencies found during internal audits?

4.18 Training
☐ Has all of the sales staff been trained and are records available?

Research, Design, Development

4.1 Management Responsibility
☐ Are the quality policy and objectives documented in the design organization?
☐ Is your organization trained and does it understand your quality policy?
☐ Are there job descriptions that define authority and responsibility within the group and at each level of review?
☐ Are designs systematically verified against specifications by parties independent of those doing the actual work?

4.2 Quality System
☐ Are there documented procedures and defined processes for the development of a design?
☐ Are your design input and output requirements defined?
☐ Do design output requirements incorporate regulatory requirements as well as crucial safety requirements?
☐ Do you have procedures for formal design review?
☐ What are your procedures for design changes?

4.3 Contract Review
☐ Do you have contract review procedures for specific customer designs?

4.4 Design Control
☐ Are organizational interfaces specific to a contract defined and are the appropriate employees aware?

❏ Are requirements available to production for inquiry?

❏ Are inputs to the design process and outputs (work leaving the design process to another group or customer) reviewed for adequacy and verified to meet customer and regulatory requirements?

❏ Has design review incorporated alternate calculations and comparisons to similar designs?

❏ Do output documents adequately define material and methods requirements?

❏ Have you validated the design to ensure it meets requirements in all intended environments?

4.5 Document and Data Control

❏ Are revisions handled to properly control changes to documents, codes, software, and standards?

❏ Are handwritten revisions dated and signed by an authorized individual and reissued within a reasonable period of time?

❏ Are there methods for the recall of a design document?

❏ Are the relevant standards (internal and external) available for review and are they handled according to your defined procedures?

4.6 Purchasing

❏ Are interfaces with procurement defined and specifications reviewed to ensure receipt of proper information?

4.8 Product Identification and Traceability

❏ Does your documentation provide for clear identification of the product and materials as well as traceability?

4.9 Process Control

❏ Does documentation provide for adequate workmanship, methods, and material acceptance instructions?

❏ Do work instructions contain adequate equipment, consumable, and environmental information?

4.10 Inspection and Testing

☐ Do adequate procurement, inspection, test instructions, documents, and records exist to ensure acquisition of required goods?

4.11 Control of Inspection, Measuring, and Test Equipment

☐ Do documented calibration procedures exist that require the identification and location of equipment?

☐ Are methods defined for calibration and revision of all equipment and software.

4.16 Control of Quality Records

☐ Are design review records maintained, retrievable, and storage adequate?

4.18 Training

☐ Are training requirements reviewed regularly for adequacy?

☐ Do all employees have training records?

4.20 Statistical Techniques

☐ Are the procedures for the application of statistical tools adequate and reviewed for effectiveness?

Planning

4.1 Management Responsibility

☐ Are your quality policy and objectives documented?

☐ Is your organization trained and does it understand your quality policy?

☐ Are there job descriptions that define authority and responsibility?

☐ Is capacity verified against contract requirements for adequacy?

☐ Are work orders and instructions verified against customer contract by those not doing the work?

4.2 Quality System
☐ Are master scheduling and work order procedures established and documented?

4.4 Design Control
☐ Are interfaces with design, production, and shipping formalized?

4.5 Document and Data Control
☐ Are procedures established for control and distribution and changing of documents?
☐ Does revision status align with documents maintained in engineering and documentation control?
☐ Are obsolete documents and schedules promptly removed?
☐ Are approved work orders released per procedures?
☐ Do you have procedures in place to ensure the proper collection and handling of the internal and external standards referenced in your designs?

4.6 Purchasing
☐ Is the interface with procurement, sales, and production documented?
☐ Are communications with subcontractors formalized to incorporate methods, specifications, and inspection, testing, and personnel qualifications?
☐ Are requisitions for subcontractors reviewed by authorized individuals for compliance to specifications?

4.7 Control of Customer Supplied Product
☐ Does the purchaser notify your organization of supply problems with materials in a formal manner? Is there a documented process for updating your planning?
☐ Are records maintained for evaluation of purchaser supplied product?

4.9 Process Control
☐ Are production schedules and activities executed according to procedures?
☐ Do work instructions include descriptions, parameters, sequences, tooling requirements, reporting, and special skills requirements?

4.10 Inspection and Testing
☐ Are the interfaces with inspection and testing and specific hold points defined as part of your planning?

4.11 Control of Inspection, Measuring, and Test Equipment
☐ Is the availability of inspection and testing equipment considered in your plan?

4.16 Control of Quality Records
☐ Are planning records maintained and easily retrievable per your documented plans and requirements?

4.18 Training
☐ Are your training requirements established and regularly reviewed?
☐ Do all of your employees have training records?

4.20 Statistical Techniques
☐ Are the procedures for the application of statistical tools reviewed for effectiveness?

Procurement

4.1 Management Responsibility
☐ Does your organization understand your quality policy?
☐ Are there job descriptions that define authority and responsibility for ensuring the proper assessment of suppliers?

4.2 Quality System
☐ Are there established procedures for subcontractor assessment and are they followed?
☐ Do these procedures incorporate inquiries and methods for source as well as receiving inspections?

4.4 Design Control
☐ Is the information stream between procurement and design documented?

4.5 Document and Data Control
☐ Are procedures for the distribution of documents, change orders, and purchase order reviews established and employees trained in their use?
☐ Is a current listing of approved suppliers available?
☐ Do drawing revisions sent to suppliers align with those in planning and engineering?
☐ Are purchase orders and changes reviewed and approved prior to being released?

4.6 Purchasing
☐ Are subcontractors selected based on records of performance as well as their business processes?
☐ Do you have a supplier rating system and a maintained listing of authorized/approved suppliers?
☐ Do the procedures define the handling of source inspections as well as the relationships between types of purchased products and inspection methods?
☐ Are your source inspection requirements specified on your purchase documents?

4.16 Control of Quality Records
☐ Are the performance and nonconformance records of the suppliers adequately maintained and reviewed?

❑ Are records of supplier audits maintained?

4.18 Training
❑ Are procurement function training records available and reviewed regularly?
❑ Is the staff competent to perform the assigned tasks?

4.20 Statistical Techniques
❑ Are sampling procedures established for suppliers that ensure product conformity?
❑ Are sample sizes taken to plan and are records used to determine the relationship with the supplier and the inspection methods used?

Stores/Materials Handling

4.1 Management Responsibility
❑ Are there job descriptions that define quality authority and responsibility?

4.2 Quality System
❑ Are monitoring and maintenance of materials procedures defined and documented?

4.5 Document and Data Control
❑ Are procedures established for the issuance of work orders and materials disbursement and for changes to these instructions?
❑ Are out-of-revision documents removed from the area?

4.6 Purchasing
❑ Are communications with purchasing formalized?
❑ Is the movement of materials to and from stores formalized, documented, and authorized?

4.9 Process Control

- ☐ Is the amount and type of materials receiving inspection clearly defined by product or type?
- ☐ Are the procedures established for reinspection of aged materials and are records maintained?
- ☐ If materials don't conform, are they separated from the normal flow and identified as nonconforming per your documented procedures?
- ☐ Are performing operators receiving inspections according to defined procedures?
- ☐ Are there procedures in place to assess the condition of stock within defined intervals?

4.12 Inspection and Test Status

- ☐ Are there methods and documents for indicating that a product or material has been satisfactorily inspected and released by the appropriate authority?

4.13 Control of Nonconforming Product

- ☐ Are there procedures for the handling and disposition of nonconforming products and materials?
- ☐ Do these procedures include responsibility for review and authorization for release?
- ☐ Do nonconforming products and materials that require corrective action remain identified as nonconforming until passing reinspection?

4.14 Corrective and Preventive Action

- ☐ Are documented investigative procedures in place to determine the cause of nonconforming materials?
- ☐ Are records of these investigations kept and have these been used for the evaluation of suppliers?
- ☐ Do you keep a record of the procedures changed due to your investigation of nonconformities?

4.15 Handling, Storage, Packaging, and Delivery

☐ Do the documented procedures include location and storage tracking, identification, handling of open packaging, handling nonconformities, FIFO inventory cycling, and storage environments?

☐ Do the methods ensure adequate environmental protection and size?

☐ Are products identified and materials handled according to shelf-life requirements?

☐ If appropriate, do you have procedures in place to support customer requests for special handling?

4.16 Control of Quality Records

☐ Are records of supplier performance, inspection, samples, nonconformance disposition, and subcontractor quality maintained per procedures and requirements?

4.20 Statistical Techniques

☐ Are sampling procedures established for materials that ensure product conformity?

☐ Are sample sizes taken to plan and are records used to determine the relationship between the materials and the inspection method used to validate effectiveness?

Production

4.1 Management Responsibility

☐ Is your organization trained to perform the production activity and does it understand your quality policy?

☐ Are there job descriptions that define quality authority and responsibility?

☐ Have you assigned and trained a person to monitor your process and product?

☐ Do your employees know your quality policy?

4.2 Quality System
☐ Are monitoring procedures for your process and products documented with acceptance characteristics and criteria?
☐ Are procedures for test and inspection documented?

4.4 Design Control
☐ Are design interfaces defined and documented?

4.5 Document and Data Control
☐ Are there procedures for the distribution and removal of documents, and are all obsolete documents removed?
☐ Do you have procedures in place to acquire and maintain external documents/standards referenced in your production processes?

4.6 Purchasing
☐ Is the removal of materials from stores by production coordinated with planning and are these methods documented in formal procedures?

4.8 Product Identification and Traceability
☐ Can operators identify all materials and products and ensure traceability throughout the entire process as defined by your procedures?

4.9 Process Control
☐ Are production schedules available?
☐ Are monitoring procedures established and results documented?
☐ Is there a documented method for determining a special process and have those areas been defined?
☐ Have operators been trained and qualified to operate process equipment and has the equipment been reviewed and approved for effectiveness?
☐ Are the environment and equipment suitable for the production tasks?

☐ Are there maintenance schedules for all key pieces of equipment and is the maintenance being performed?

4.10 Inspection and Testing

☐ Is the relationship between inspection and monitoring clearly defined to include intervals, amount, and frequency?

☐ Are all products inspected prior to release, and are nonconforming products held or separated from the process?

☐ Are nonconforming products clearly identified and remain so until a plan of action is completed and the material undergoes a full reinspection?

4.11 Control of Inspection, Measuring, and Test Equipment

☐ Do the inspection and test criteria also include the equipment and software to be used?

☐ Does the test equipment have a calibration indicator of the current status?

☐ Are these tools and indicators safeguarded from unauthorized adjustments?

4.12 Inspection and Test Status

☐ Do inspection procedures require the identification of test status by marking, location, or supporting documents?

☐ Is there a formally designated individual/group responsible for determination and action related to nonconforming products or materials?

4.13 Control of Nonconforming Product

☐ Are there procedures for the handling and disposition of nonconforming products?

☐ Do these procedures include responsibility for review and authorization for release?

☐ Do nonconforming products that require corrective action remain identified as nonconforming until reinspection is complete?

4.14 Corrective and Preventive Action

☐ Do you have documented procedures that call for the investigation of nonconforming products or materials?

☐ Can you demonstrate how your corrective action process has resulted in the changing of your processes and procedures and how it has been effective in preventing nonconformances?

4.15 Handling, Storage, Packaging, and Delivery

☐ Are there formal procedures established for the effective preservation and protection of materials used in production?

☐ Are these materials preserved and dispatched according to these procedures?

4.16 Control of Quality Records

☐ Are monitoring, inspection, test, sample, process equipment, personnel, process analysis, production activities, and nonconformance records maintained as required by your quality policy and customer contracts?

☐ Are these records easy to retrieve?

4.18 Training

☐ Are production employee training records reviewed regularly to ensure adequacy and conformance?

☐ Are those employees who are involved in special processes fully qualified with supporting training documents?

☐ Do all your employees comply with the background or education requirements as you have defined in your training requirements?

4.20 Statistical Techniques

☐ Are sampling procedures established for materials that adequately ensure product conformance?

☐ Are procedures established to verify that the process being used is in control?

☐ Have you performed a review of the areas for potential statistical applications?

Inspection

4.1 Management Responsibility
☐ Are there functional job descriptions that define quality authority and responsibility?
☐ Is there a formal organization established for in-house audits that is adequately staffed and trained?

4.3 Contract Review
☐ Are contract review procedures established that ensure the availability of information and the validation of the contract?
☐ Are records retained to support the contract review activity?

4.4 Design Control
☐ Are design interfaces defined and documented?

4.5 Document and Data Control
☐ Are your procedures reviewed and authorized by the appropriate personnel?
☐ Do you have documentation control procedures that ensure the availability of current documents at the appropriate locations and the removal of obsolete revision documents?
☐ Are changes approved by an authorized individual and identified through a revision document?

4.6 Purchasing
☐ Are there procedures in place to support source inspections?

4.8 Product Identification and Traceability
☐ Are there procedures for identification of the material/product through the entire production process?

4.9 Process Control
☐ Are procedures/work instructions available in areas where quality depends on them?

☐ Are these procedures/work instructions being followed?

☐ Are special processes identified and are there methods in place to ensure that they are being reviewed?

4.10 Inspection and Testing

☐ Are procedures in place for effective incoming material inspection and documentation?

☐ Are materials held until they are identified as acceptable for production?

☐ Do you have defined procedures for allowing nonverified materials into production with the proper authorization identified?

☐ Are nonconforming products segregated from the flow and positively identified?

☐ Are there procedures for verification of materials during inspection?

☐ Are all appropriate inspection documents completed prior to the material being released?

☐ Are all inspection records and documents properly maintained?

☐ Do your inspection records identify who released the product?

4.11 Control of Inspection, Measuring, and Test Equipment

☐ Do the inspection and test criteria include the equipment and software to be used, and are these appropriate for the task defined?

☐ When performing inspection, are the appropriate materials and equipment available, and are they maintained to the correct precision as defined by your calibration program?

☐ Does the test equipment have an indicator of the current calibration status?

☐ Are these tools and indicators safeguarded from unauthorized adjustments?

☐ Do you perform a reinspection when your testing equipment is found to be out of calibration or malfunctioning?

☐ Can you produce records to prove the reinspection?

☐ Are methods established for the proper care and storage of test equipment and software?

☐ Are regular checks performed on the test equipment and software to verify conformance?

4.12 Inspection and Test Status

☐ Do inspection procedures require the identification of test status by marking, locating, or supporting documents?

☐ Is there a formally designated individual/group responsible for determining nonconforming products or materials?

4.13 Control of Nonconforming Product

☐ Are there procedures for the handling and disposition of nonconforming products?

☐ Do these procedures include responsibility for review and authorization for release?

☐ Do all nonconforming products that require corrective action remain identified as nonconforming until reinspection is complete?

4.14 Corrective and Preventive Action

☐ Do you have documented procedures that call for the investigation of nonconforming products, materials, or processes?

☐ Can you demonstrate how your corrective action process has changed inspection processes and procedures and has been effective in preventing nonconformances?

4.16 Control of Quality Records

☐ Are monitoring, inspection, test, sample, and nonconformance records maintained as required by your quality policy and customer contracts?

4.18 Training

☐ Are those employees who are involved in inspection processes fully qualified with supporting training documents?

4.20 Statistical Techniques
☐ Do you have procedures for identifying acceptable statistical methods to be employed for inspection?

Shipping/Transport

4.1 Management Responsibility
☐ Are your quality policy and objectives documented?
☐ Does the organization understand your quality policy?
☐ Are there job descriptions that define authority and responsibility for verifying the quality of the shipping/transport work being performed?
☐ Are requirements for the verification of shipment accuracy available in the area?

4.3 Contract Review
☐ Are contract requirements for shipment defined and met?
☐ Is verification of compliance documented and retained?

4.5 Document and Data Control
☐ Are elements of the transfer documents forwarded to the appropriate parties?
☐ Do you readily remove obsolete documents from the areas?

4.8 Product Identification and Traceability
☐ Are procedures in place to ensure traceability?
☐ Are your products marked per your requirements?

4.12 Inspection and Test Status
☐ Do you maintain procedures for the verification of requirements, and are the verification records easily available?

4.15 Handling, Storage, Packaging, and Delivery
☐ Have you developed a comprehensive set of procedures

addressing handling, storage, packaging, postinspection, and test handling and delivery availability?

☐ Do you have procedures in place to address special customer handling requirements?

4.16 Control of Quality Records

☐ Do your procedures identify the proper handling, sorting, and storage of shipping records?

☐ Are these records easily retrieved and are they accurate?

4.18 Training

☐ Are employee training records reviewed regularly to ensure adequacy and conformance?

☐ Are employees who are involved in the physical movement of materials fully qualified with supporting training documents?

Servicing

4.1 Management Responsibility

☐ Are your quality policy and objectives documented?

☐ Is your organization trained and does it understand your quality policy?

☐ Are there job descriptions that define authority and responsibility for servicing?

☐ Is there a formal organization established for in-house auditing that is adequately staffed and trained?

4.3 Contract Review

☐ Are there procedures established to support customer inquiries?

☐ Are the requirements for service contracts defined?

☐ Are order preparation and review procedures established to ensure customers' requests can be satisfied?

☐ Are methods established for clarification of orders with customers?

☐ Are there verification procedures to ensure proper translation of customer orders into internal work orders?

☐ Are communications to customers formalized?

4.5 Document and Data Control

☐ Are your service procedures reviewed and authorized by the appropriate personnel?

☐ Do you have documentation control procedures that ensure the availability of current documents at the appropriate locations and the removal of obsolete documents?

☐ Are changes to documents approved by an authorized individual and identified through a revision document?

4.8 Product Identification and Traceability

☐ Do you have formal methods and procedures for the anticipation and identification of needed spare parts?

4.9 Process Control

☐ Do you have procedures that clearly identify methods for the establishment of servicing schedules and results?

☐ Have you identified any special processes and qualified the individuals to perform the task and inspections?

☐ Are the correct work instructions and equipment available for those performing the tasks?

4.10 Inspection and Testing

☐ Do you have inspection and test procedures for all the products you service?

4.11 Control of Inspection, Measuring, and Test Equipment

☐ Do the inspection and test criteria include the equipment and software to be used, and are they appropriate for the task defined?

☐ When performing inspection, are the appropriate materials and equipment available, and are they maintained to the correct precision as defined by your calibration program?

☐ Does the test equipment have an indicator of the current calibration status?

☐ Are these tools and indicators safeguarded from unauthorized adjustments?

☐ Do you perform a reinspection when your testing equipment is found to be out of calibration or malfunctioning?

☐ Can you produce records to prove the reinspection?

☐ Are methods established for the proper care and storage of the test equipment and software?

☐ Are regular checks performed on the test equipment and software to verify conformance?

4.12 Inspection and Test Status

☐ Do inspection procedures require the identification of test status by marking, location, or supporting documents?

☐ Is there a formally designated individual or group responsible for determination and action related to nonconforming products or materials?

4.13 Control of Nonconforming Product

☐ Are there procedures for the handling and disposition of nonconforming products?

☐ Do these procedures include responsibility for review and authorization for release?

☐ Do nonconforming products that require corrective action remain identified as nonconforming until inspection is complete?

☐ Are nonconforming products separated and remain identified as nonconforming until final disposition?

4.14 Corrective and Preventive Action

☐ Do you have procedures in place to collect and analyze customer complaints?

☐ Are customer complaints analyzed and responded to based on the degree of risk?

☐ Are corrective actions recorded and their referenced procedures corrected?

4.15 Handling, Storage, Packaging, and Delivery

☐ Have you developed a comprehensive set of procedures addressing handling, storage, packaging, postinspection, and test handling and delivery availability?

4.16 Control of Quality Records

☐ Do your records include repair activities, customer complaints, test equipment calibration records, products you support, and the cause of a breakdown for corrective action?

4.18 Training

☐ Are training records of service employees reviewed regularly to ensure adequacy and conformance?

☐ Can you ensure that employees trained on only specific equipment work on only that equipment?

4.19 Servicing

☐ Do your procedures require verification that your actions met the specified requirements?

4.20 Statistical Techniques

☐ Have you performed a review of your operations for potential applications of statistical tools?

Appendix 2

Sample Quality Manual

The Global Competitor's Sample Quality Manual
Table of Contents

Note: This quality manual is available on disk, see page 201.

Section: **1.0**	Date Issued:

Element: **Quality Policy**

Revision:	Authorized By:	Approved By:

1.0 Quality Policy

It is the policy of the company to design, fabricate, market, distribute, and service products with consistently high quality such that they will reliably perform their intended function result in recognition as a quality leader in the industry.

All of our products will be consistent with the public good, meet all applicable laws and regulations.

_____ Date ____/____/____
President

Section: **2.0**	Date Issued:	
Element: **Authorization**		
Revision:	Authorized By:	Approved By:

2.0 Authorization

This manual is published to identify minimum business process requirements. This document serves as a summary of the responsibilities and activities that will allow us to meet the requirements of the ISO 9000 standard.

The fundamental concept of this document is to provide procedural information appropriate for the activity necessary for instruction and control over all operations affecting quality. It is the intention of this manual to provide guidance for each area within the company, to ensure they develop systems, procedures, keep records, and provide evidence of successful testing and internal audits of processes, people, and products.

This document will be controlled and maintained by the following people:

1. President
2. General Manager
3. Vice President of Engineering
4. Vice President of Production
5. Production Manager
6. Quality Control Manager
7. Shipping Supervisor
8. Order processing Supervisor
9. Sales Manager
10. Personnel Manager
11. Materials Manager
12. Service Manager

This entire manual will be reviewed no later than every two years, and sections will be updated when necessary to appropriately reflect the quality plan for our company. A record of these updates has been retained by the quality control manager.

This manual has been authorized by:

_____ Date ____/____/____
President
_____ Date ____/____/____
Quality Control Manager

Section: **3.0**	Date Issued:
Element: **Introduction**	
Revision: Authorized By:	Approved By:

3.0 Introduction

This company was founded in _ _ _ _ (specify date) . We have facilities in _ _ _
_ (locations) and we manufacture the following products _ _ _ _ (product classes)
in these facilities. Our primary business is the _ _ _ _ (general categories) markets.
We do our designs in the _ _ _ _ (location) and receive our orders at those locations.

*Note: you want to try and give your auditors a general description of how your orders
flow through your operations and under whose control. An organization chart is also
advised here with titles only.*

Section: **4.1**	Date Issued:
Element: **Management Responsibility**	
Revision: Authorized By:	Approved By:

4.1 Management Responsibility

4.1.1 Scope
It is the intent of this section to properly identify responsibility for ensuring that both ISO 9000 and our quality policy requirements are met.

4.1.1.1 Our Quality Policy is defined in Section 1 of this manual.

4.1.2 Responsibility and Authority
The quality control program within this company has been established at the direction of the president. The responsibility for the development and integration of the quality plan resides within the quality control operation.

The responsibility for execution of the quality program is delegated to the operational managers. The operational managers may delegate responsibility for the quality program, however they will maintain the ultimate responsibility.

The quality control manager oversees the quality control operations for the company as shown in Figure 4.1.2-a. The quality control operation has the responsibility for overseeing, incoming material inspection, in-process test, final inspection, and statistical techniques in conjunction with the operating departments. Audits shall be conducted directly by quality control.

Quality control has the organizational freedom and authority to initiate action to prevent the occurrence of nonconformities, record problems, initiate corrective actions, verify solutions, and if necessary, stop those processes until such time as they fully comply.

4.1.3 Resources
Each organization shall designate appropriately trained individuals, to meet all the requirements of the quality program. Personnel performing these quality inspections shall be approved by quality control.

Incoming material inspection shall verify the conformance of incoming raw materials and products against the design specifications and will be managed by the materials organization and overseen by quality control.

In-process inspection, final inspection, and functional testing shall ensure conformance to product design specification. This function will be managed by production and overseen by quality control.

Section: **4.1**	Date Issued:
Element: **Management Responsibility**	
Revision:	Authorized By:	Approved By:

Design reviews will be initiated and conducted by all appropriately designated personnel. This function shall be managed by engineering and overseen by quality control

Internal quality audits of processes and products used to verify conformance shall be performed by independent personnel trained and appointed by the quality control organization. Personnel performing the quality audits can audit any area for which they are trained and where they do not have responsibility for the products or service being produced there.

4.1.4 Management Representative

The quality control manager is responsible for ensuring that the ISO 9000 requirements are met as well as all other customer requested requirements. It is also the function of the quality control manager to provide regular feedback on the status of the quality system and its progress. This will be accomplished via a quarterly report on those measures reflective of the quality system.

The quality control manager will also act as the primary communications point with reference to any outside bodies affecting the quality system.

4.1.5 Management Review

During each calendar year, the quality control manager shall review the quality system's methodology and its application to the ISO 9000 Standard. Revisions to the manual and quality system shall be made as required to guarantee the quality of the product, services, and the needs of the company.

The president and staff will conduct regular reviews of quality issues. These reviews will result in corrective plans. Reviews and actions will be reflected in the minutes of those meetings.

Section: **4.2**		Date Issued:
Element: **Quality System**		
Revision:	Authorized By:	Approved By:

4.2 Quality System

4.2.1 Scope

This section provides an outline of the quality control program as a means for ensuring that the products and processes conform to the specified requirements of the customer requirements and the ISO 9000 standard. This outline is captured in this quality manual. It is the responsibility of the quality control manager to maintain this manual as an outline as well as this document of our overall quality plan. A detailed listing of procedures supporting this plan for all areas is listed in Appendix 4.2.1.A.

4.2.2 Quality System

The quality control program is a formally documented system of planned activities established to provide evidence of compliance to the requirements of applicable regulations, codes, standards, contractual specifications, drawings, ISO 9000, as well as the company quality policy.

All of these activities are governed by procedures and written instructions supported with records of training and satisfactory compliance of products and processes.

The operational managers shall establish measures to implement these requirements as defined in this manual. This shall include the preparation of procedures and documentation that will assure compliance to the quality control program.

4.2.3 Quality Planning

This quality manual and all the supporting departmental procedures shall be referred to as the quality plan.

The preparation of the plan shall be the responsibility of the quality control organization and those individual organizations affected by the ISO 9000 standard and maintained in conjunction with senior managements review, that shall take place at least every two years.

The identification of controls and equipment needed to ensure conformance to customer requirements is the responsibility of the organizations assigned to the immediate task.

Section: **4.2**	Date Issued:
Element: **Quality System**	
Revision:	Authorized By:	Approved By:

Ensuring that designs are appropriate to the requirements, the testing criteria, development of test equipment, and the ability to meet design completion dates is the responsibility of the engineering organization.

The identification of suitable verification points and clarification of those acceptability standards within the manufacturing process shall be the responsibility of Production.

The responsibility for identification, preparation, and maintenance of records shall remain with the organization that is performing the tasks.

Section: **4.3**	Date Issued:
Element: **Contract Review**	
Revision: Authorized By:	Approved By:

4.3 Contract Review

4.3.1 Scope

This section provides for the process by which we establish and maintain procedures for the acceptance and review of customer orders. It will also address the coordination of all follow-up activities. This process shall be the responsibility of the sales organization to ensure documented procedures and records are in place to adequately meet the requirements of ISO 9000.

4.3.2 Review

The sales organization will maintain a documented system with appropriately maintained records to ensure the appropriate review of the customers orders. This shall include ensuring that the order is well understood by both parties and that we have the capability to meet the requirement. These procedures require agreement prior to the acceptance to the order. It is the responsibility of the sales organization to ensure a comprehensive documented integration of this requirement exists.

4.3.3 Amendments to Contracts

Each organization affected shall maintain procedures for the processes used to amend a customer requirement to ensure compliance with the request.

4.3.4 Records

The customer orders (contracts) shall be maintained by the sales organization for the duration of the warranty period plus one year unless otherwise requested by the customer. Documented procedures shall exist to support the retention of these records.

Section: 4.4	Date Issued:
Element: **Design Control**	
Revision: Authorized By:	Approved By:

4.4 Design Control

4.4.1 Scope
It is the responsibility of the engineering organization to maintain documented procedures to control and verify the design of the product in order to ensure that specified requirements are met. This documented system shall begin with the initial design and carry through to the final product validation.

4.4.2 Design and Development Planning
Engineering must plan and document each development project. Each design activity will have its responsibility, resources, and qualified relationships defined. As the development project progresses, the plan for the project will be reviewed and approved by qualified individuals.

4.4.3 Organizational and Technical Interfaces
The engineering organization is responsible for ensuring that they receive all the appropriate specifications from our customers, the marketing organization, as well as any required outside standards. They shall maintain a documented process that ensures collection of this information and that it is integrated into the design review process.

4.4.4 Design Input
Engineering is required to ensure a documented process that requires an investigation into all the regulatory requirements that affect the design as well as any customer requirements. They are also required to ensure that any ambiguities with the design are resolved with the appropriate parties. The design input reviews must be documented and maintained by the engineering organization for a period of ___ years.

4.4.5 Design Review
Engineering shall ensure that as the design evolves, there are recorded reviews of the documented design by individuals affected by the design.

Section: **4.4**	Date Issued:
Element: **Design Control**	
Revision: Authorized By:	Approved By:

4.4.6 Design Output

Engineering shall ensure that the designs are documented in a form that can be readily verified to meet the design input requirements, that test acceptance criteria specified, and that assembly and safe operating instructions are included.

The designs shall be reviewed and approved by a senior engineering manager prior to release.

4.4.7 Design Verification

The design will undergo verification by the appropriate engineering personnel to ensure it meets the criteria of the design plan. When appropriate, they will conduct recorded performance calculations, comparisons with prior products, and appropriate demonstrations prior to the release of the design.

4.4.8 Design Validation

Upon completion and release of the design, a prototype of the product will undergo a documented review to ensure the product performs to customer specifications in the operating environment intended.

4.4.9 Design Changes

All changes to the design will undergo a formal design change review that ensures the appropriate review by identified parties in the original design plan. Should the product exist prior to a design plan requirement, or the scope of the change is restricted or limited, then the engineering manager will identify those affected parties. No changes shall be made without a design change review.

Section: 4.5	Date Issued:
Element: Document and Data Control	
Revision: Authorized By:	Approved By:

4.5 Document and Data Control

4.5.1 Scope

It is the responsibility of each organization to establish and maintain the control of all the documents, instructions, and data in their operations to meet the intent of the ISO 9000 standard. It is also the responsibility of each organization that calls for standards that exist outside of the organization to maintain procedures for their collection, maintenance, and distribution.

4.5.2 Documentation Approval and Issue

Each organization is responsible for the establishment and maintenance of the documents. Documents and Instructions must be established whenever a lack there of could adversely affect the quality of the process, product, or services provided by that operation. The individual organizations are responsible to ensure that these documents are approved by the supervision of the area, an authorized technical individual who can evaluate the process and methods used to meet the requirements of the design, and finally the employees performing the task. In the case of conducting tests, the quality control organization's approved representative shall also be required to approve the document.

Each individual organization will maintain the procedures/instructions/documents within the user organization such that each employee who is performing the task can easily retrieve the documents for reference. These instructions/documents can take many physical forms. We do not require a single format, however these documents must be controlled, contain a control number, revision, issuance date, a reference to the ISO 9000 standard elements addressed, and the appropriate signatures.

A master revision listing of the documents are maintained and issued by the quality control organization, however the master document is generated and maintained by the user organization. It is the responsibility of the user organization to ensure that only current documents are available for usage. Obsolete documents must be promptly removed by the department and adequately identified as available for reference only.

Section: **4.5**		Date Issued:
Element: **Document and Data Control**		
Revision:	Authorized By:	Approved By:

4.5.3 Document Changes

Prior to the issuance of any new procedures/instructions/documents the same approval requirements exist. To upgrade a document, the quality control organization must be requested to provide a new revision number for update into the document matrix. When making changes, it is requested that the changes from the previous instruction be highlighted to ensure the proper changes are readily implemented.

Section: **4.6**	Date Issued:
Element: **Purchasing**	
Revision: Authorized By:	Approved By:

4.6 Purchasing

4.6.1 Scope

The purchasing organization shall establish and maintain a documented process with appropriate records that ensure the purchased products meet defined specifications and the requirements of ISO 9000.

4.6.2 Evaluation of the Suppliers

The purchasing organization shall establish documented procedures by which a supplier is selected. The selection shall incorporate at least three considerations in the following order or priority: 1) their ability to deliver material that meets the product specifications, 2) the evaluation of their quality organization to ensure consistent delivery of all requirements, and 3) a cost competitive delivery of the material.

The purchasing organization in conjunction with the quality control organization shall determine the methodology employed to ensure the receipt of the appropriately conforming materials.

The purchasing organization in conjunction with the incoming materials inspection organization shall maintain records of the suppliers performance. The purchasing organization shall only purchase materials from approved suppliers. It is the responsibility of the purchasing organization to establish and maintain procedures for the generation of an acceptable supplier listing. The listings of approved suppliers must have the approval of the quality control organization.

4.6.3 Purchasing Data

The purchase orders provided to our suppliers will contain appropriate information that clearly defines the product and quality needed and the delivery requirement. When appropriate we will include additional requirements such as workmanship, content, and inspection criteria.

Section: 4.6		Date Issued:
Element: **Purchasing**		
Revision:	Authorized By:	Approved By:

4.6.4 Verification of Purchased Product

The purchasing organization shall define how they will ensure that all materials introduced into the operations have undergone a review for conformity. The purchasing organization will look at materials by commodity grouping and define inspection routines for each commodity. The receipt history of the supplier shall play a large role in determining the inspection status and can cause an exception within the commodity. Where exceptions are warranted, a separate inspection methodology will be defined. When a source inspection is indicated, it will be specified in the purchase document. With the completion of a source inspection, the material will be brought into our operations with the understanding that it may be rejected at any time it is found to be nonconforming.

Records of the supplier's performance shall be available should our customers request them.

Section: 4.7	Date Issued:
Element: **Control of Customer Supplied Product**	
Revision: Authorized By:	Approved By:

4.7 Control of Customer Supplied Product

4.7.1 Scope

When a customer provides materials for our usage or integration into another material, it shall be controlled in the same manner as our own existing materials. It is the responsibility of the materials organization to communicate the status of the materials provided to the sales organization as requested. The materials organization shall establish procedures for such tracking and communications.

Section: **4.8**	Date Issued:

Element: **Product Identification and Traceability**		

Revision:	Authorized By:	Approved By:

4.8 Product Identification and Traceability

4.8.1 Scope

The materials organization shall be responsible for ensuring the identification of all materials as they move through the manufacturing process. This responsibility shall require the creation and maintenance of procedures and records that accurately identify and report the status of the materials. These procedures will be generated in conjunction with the departments that handle the materials. These procedures shall incorporate traceability of components to meet our customers requirements, along with the appropriate recording of batches.

The materials organization is also responsible for the recording of implemented engineering changes to the product lines.

Section: **4.9**		Date Issued:
Element: **Process Control**		
Revision:	Authorized By:	Approved By:

4.9 Process Control

4.9.1 Scope

It is the responsibility of each organizational group to develop and maintain controlled process that ensure their continued conformance to customer requirement and the ISO 9000 standard. This includes operating instructions for all organizations and employees that affect quality. Specific work instructions are required where a lack there of could adversely affect quality.

We believe a controlled process includes:

- a. Documented work instructions/procedures that define the manner of production, installation, and servicing.
- b. Use of suitable production and installation equipment.
- c. Suitable working environment.,
- d. Compliance with referenced standards/codes and quality plans.
- e. Monitoring and control of suitable process and product characteristics during design and production.
- f. Approval of process and equipment as appropriate.
- g. The criteria for workmanship is stipulated in the clearest modes possible.
- h. There is suitable maintenance of equipment to assure continued capability.

Occasionally we will engage in processes that are not immediately verifiable. When such special processes do exist, each organization will identify these processes and initiate a continuous monitoring of the key parameters affecting the workmanship. Additionally the operators will undergo specific training and qualification for that process. Each organization will develop procedures and retain specific records for these special processes.

The use and extent of work instructions shall be balanced such that an extensive training program and records can be used to reduce the detail of the work instruction where practical.

It is recommended that where possible the assembly instructions follow a "box and diamond" flow charting method, however it is not required.

Section: **4.10**	Date Issued:
Element: Inspection and Testing	
Revision: Authorized By:	Approved By:

4.10 Inspection and Testing

4.10.1 Scope

Each organization will establish and maintain documented procedures for the inspection and testing activities associated with the verification of specific requirements of the materials/product. They will also maintain the appropriate supporting records demonstrating compliance as described in the department's procedures. All will meet the ISO 9000 requirements. If the materials need to forgo the defined inspection routines, then a "positive recall" should be invoked. This documented procedure shall require the tracking of this material to support its recall. No material may be released to the customer without the completion of all functional design and safety requirements testing.

All procedures and activities affecting testing shall be overseen by Quality Control and their signature on the proposed procedures is required. All test criteria will be based upon the output requirements generated by the Engineering organization.

4.10.2 Receiving Inspection and Testing:

It is the responsibility of the Materials organization and the Incoming Materials Inspection Department to ensure that no materials are used until they can verify compliance with the specified materials requirements. These inspections shall be carried out according to documented inspection procedures with the appropriate records retained and in conjunction with Purchasing's inspection plans for the materials. These testing procedures shall carry Quality Control's approval.

4.10.3 In-Process Inspection and Testing

The Production organization must generate a comprehensive inspection and test plan that ensures that all the defined testing requirements are met. This testing plan must include documented testing instructions, the retention of records that support the conformance of the product, and who is authorized to conduct such tests. No materials may bypass these inspection plans or continue to be processed without successful completion of the test requirements. These in process testing procedures shall carry Quality Control's approval.

Section: **4.10**	Date Issued:

Element: **Inspection and Testing**

Revision:	Authorized By:	Approved By:

4.10.4 Final Inspection and Testing

The production organization must generate a comprehensive inspection and test plan that ensures that all the defined testing requirements are met. This testing plan must include documented testing instructions, the retention of records that support the conformance of the product, and who is authorized to conduct such tests. No materials may bypass these inspection points or continue to be processed without successful completion of the test requirements. These final testing procedures shall carry quality control's approval.

4.10.5 Inspection and Test Records

Each organization will retain records that are easily retrievable for inspection by our customers, should they desire proof of compliance. These records will be retained for the warranty period plus one year by production.

Section: **4.11**	Date Issued:
Element: **Control of Inspection, Measuring, and Test Equipment**	
Revision: Authorized By:	Approved By:

4.11 Control of Inspection, Measuring, and Test Equipment

4.11.1 Scope

Each organization will establish and maintain documented procedures to select, control, calibrate, and maintain inspection, measuring, and test equipment used to demonstrate conformance to the specifications required. These devices include measurement tools, dyes, gauges, verification software, or any other "device" used to ensure conformance to a requirement.

All devices, once selected, shall all be routed to the calibration crib within production, prior to their use and assigned a control number and a file established. Each file will identify the tools, calibration method, acceptance criteria, usage locations, maintenance schedule as well as the calibration standard traceable back to a national standard. The devices will be reissued to the appropriate department and recalled for recalibration at predetermined intervals by the calibration crib. A full calibration history of the device shall be maintained and available to our customers when requested.

When calibration devices are brought in from outside firms (rented), and they are calibrated by the outside firm, we shall still maintain a file on them. However, we will maintain the outside organizations certification traceable back to a national standard.

No employee may maintain their own calibration devices outside of our calibration program.

4.11.2 Control Procedure

a. The production organization in conjunction with engineering approval shall determine the measurement to be made, the accuracy required and the appropriate device that is capable of the necessary precision. This record will be maintained in the device's calibration file.

b. All the devices shall have a calibration schedule established based on usage or duration of time. Where appropriate a bronze quick reference check standard will be made available in the work areas for daily quick calibration checks for such devices as calipers and micrometers. These bronze standards should also carry a calibration schedule. The calibration schedule shall call for a range of

Section: **4.11**	Date Issued:
Element: **Control of Inspection, Measuring, and Test Equipment**	
Revision: Authorized By:	Approved By:

recall such that the organizations affected will have the opportunity to respond without disrupting operations. No department shall hold a tool beyond the calibration recall date.

c. Documented inspection procedures should exist for the calibration of equipment. This should include maintenance, duration between recalls, as well as the actual testing. The procedures should also include notification of the affected departments when a device fails to meet calibration requirements.

d. All the calibration devices must carry an identification indicator noting its calibration status. Should a measurement device not be under calibration control and could possibly be used to verify the acceptance of a material, it must be clearly marked/identified that this device is not to be used for verification purposes.

e. All records of calibration shall be maintained in the calibration file.

f. Those departments notified of a calibration failure will be required to maintain a documented procedure to reverify all affected materials.

g. All departments must ensure that the environment in which the test is conducted is suitable for effective testing.

h. Management must ensure that the calibration devices are handled properly and protected when not in use. It is expected that if the tool is not being used in the immediate future, the tool will be returned back to the calibration crib for safe storage. Maintenance of the device will occur at the time of calibration or when specifically required according to the operating instructions within the device's folder.

i. No employee shall make unauthorized adjustments to calibrated devices. This instruction shall be included in the training instructions for the proper operation of the equipment. In all cases, management should set aside secure areas for calibration devices when not in immediate use.

Section: **4.12**	Date Issued:
Element: **Inspection and Test Status**	
Revision: Authorized By:	Approved By:

4.12 Inspection and Test Status

4.12.1 Scope

All materials/products shall carry an identification of their test status to ensure compliance with the desired conformance requirements. It is the responsibility of the production organization to create a documented process with procedures for ensuring that all materials/products carry a test status.

The incoming materials inspection group shall use a materials transfer tag designating transfer to raw stores for acceptable materials, or the Materials Review Board (MRB) cage for non conforming materials. In both cases the transfer tag stays with the materials.

The in process inspection stations will demonstrate compliance with a personalized inspection stamp approval on the underside of the material or a placement into the segregated reject area with no stamp.

Final inspection and test shall validate the existence of all inspection stamps against the check sheet as well as the test data and sign off on acceptance. This check sheet shall act as a quality record. Should the material fail the test or not have all the appropriate stamps then the material/product is placed in the reject area for disposition with a reject tag. The check sheet is retained for future reference (see 4.13, control of nonconforming materials).

Section: **4.13**	Date Issued:
Element: **Control of Nonconforming Product**	
Revision: Authorized By:	Approved By:

4.13 Control of Nonconforming Product

4.13.1 Scope

The appropriate organizations shall initiate and maintain procedures with the appropriate records to ensure that noncomplying materials are prevented from inadvertent use. These procedures concerning nonconforming materials shall ensure the proper identification, documentation, evaluation, segregation (when practical), disposition, and notification of affected parties such as the materials organization.

4.13.2 Nonconforming Product Review and Disposition

When a material is found to be defective/nonconforming then procedures must be in place for appropriate disposition. The authority for disposition is the Materials Review Board (MRB). The MRB will convene weekly (or sooner if need is identified) and consists of a representative from production, purchasing, engineering, and quality control. The engineering representative will provide final approval for disposition.

Disposition shall entail a thorough investigation of the defect the result of which can fall into one of the following categories.

    a. Reject or scrap

    b. Regrade to alternative applications

    c. Use as is (UAI)

    d. Rework to specified requirements (note: this material must remain identified as defective until fully reworked and reinspected).

All decisions by the board will result from an investigation of the material specifications. Any compromises to the materials will require the appropriate engineering change design approvals. All final disposition will require notification of the affected parties. In the case of a regrade to the customer's requirement, the customer must be notified and approval given prior to release.

Section: 4.14	Date Issued:
Element: **Corrective and Preventive Action**	
Revision: Authorized By:	Approved By:

4.14 Corrective and Preventive Action

4.14.1 Scope

Each appropriate organization must establish and maintain procedures for implementing corrective and preventive actions. These nonconformities shall be collected, analyzed, and root-cause corrected. The order in which they are addressed shall depend on the risks associated with the nonconformities. Safety issues shall always receive top priority and immediate allocations of resources.

In all cases where a corrective or preventative action is employed, a record of the changes made shall be recorded and the record maintained for a five-year period.

4.14.2 Corrective Action

A corrective action will result from a customer complaint or a report of a product nonconformance. These reports shall be collected via a Customer Action Request (CAR) process. The CARs may be initiated by any customer or employee and submitted to the sales organization. The sales organization will maintain a documented process by which the complaints are compiled, analyzed, and corrective action initiated and tracked. This corrective action will address not only the root cause but also the application of controls to ensure its effectiveness. These corrective and preventive actions will be executed by those organizations identified as the root cause source of the nonconformity. A report of the corrective actions taken will be reviewed by the affected senior management.

4.14.3 Preventive Action

A preventive action will result from information indicating a nonconformity within the operating process that affects quality. This information may be gathered by way of internal audits, quality records, yield shortfalls, service reports, customer complaints, or any other areas indicating process failures. These failure/shortfalls will be collected via the Quality Corrective Action Request (QCAR) system, administered by the quality control organization. The quality control organization will maintain a documented process by which the shortfalls are compiled, analyzed and preventive action initiated and tracked. This preventive action will address not only the root cause but also the application of controls to ensure its effectiveness. A report of the corrective actions taken will be reviewed by the affected senior management.

Section: **4.15**	Date Issued:
Element: **Handling, Storage, Packaging, Preservation, and Delivery**	
Revision: Authorized By:	Approved By:

4.15 Handling, Storage, Packaging, Preservation and Delivery

4.15.1 Scope
The materials organization shall establish and maintain documented procedures for the handling, storage, packaging, preservation, and delivery of products to our customers.

4.15.2 Handling
Procedures shall exist with the appropriately trained employees to ensure the proper and safe handling of materials. All forklift drivers shall attend driver training and carry a current operator's license.

4.15.3 Storage
Procedures shall exist with the appropriately trained employees to ensure the proper and safe storage of materials. All materials shall be stored to prevent deterioration as well as support easy retrieval for usage. It is the company's policy to follow a "First In-First Out" (FIFO) inventory policy and all material storage procedures shall accommodate this policy.

Those materials that are sensitive to environmental and storage duration shall have procedures that ensure their proper handling, continual monitoring, and removal if appropriate. All other materials should be monitored at regular intervals to detect deterioration.

Methods for receipts, storage, and dispatches of materials from storage areas shall occur according to documented and maintained procedures.

4.15.4 Packaging
The materials organization shall package materials and mark the containers to the appropriate engineering specifications. Operators shall be trained to the packaging instructions required.

Section: **4.15**	Date Issued:

Element: **Handling, Storage, Packaging, Preservation, and Delivery**		

Revision:	Authorized By:	Approved By:

4.15.5 Preservation

A secure area will be established to segregate the finished product to ensure its preservation. "Finished goods" materials are subject the same storage and handling requirements as those within the raw materials areas.

4.15.6 Delivery

The shipping department shall ensure appropriate consolidation, protection and shipment of a customer order to the customer's requirements. Should a customer request a "No partials" shipment, then shipment shall not occur without a documented request by the customer. All appropriate information should be loaded into the computer within the day of shipment according to documented procedures.

Section: 4.16	Date Issued:
Element: **Control of Quality Records**	
Revision: Authorized By:	Approved By:

4.16 Control of Quality Records

4.16.1 Scope

All appropriate organizations must establish and maintain documented procedures on how they handle quality records. These procedures must identify the record, method for collection, indexing, accessing, filing, storage, maintenance, and disposition. The purpose of these records is to demonstrate conformance to the specified requirements of our quality system and therefore must be legible, easily retrievable and preserved for a period at least one year beyond warranty, unless requested by our customers or where otherwise specified such as in the case of Audit records. These records shall also include assessment records of our suppliers and be available to our customers upon request.

Section: **4.17**		Date Issued:
Element: **Internal Quality Audits**		
Revision:	Authorized By:	Approved By:

4.17 Internal Quality Audits

4.17.1 Scope

The quality control organization shall establish and maintain documented procedures for the planning and implementation of internal quality audits of our business operations and the results generated.

The audits will compare actual practices to the documented procedures and instructions maintained by the organizations. They will audit all areas affecting quality to assess the degree of compliance and effectiveness of the quality system.

These audits will be conducted according to an audit plan based on the importance of the operations to the quality system, by individuals independent of those operations being audited. It is our policy that no area shall go more than one year between audits.

The audit will be conducted by trained auditors who follow the ISO 10011 standard series, Guidance on quality system audits. A listing of approved auditors will be maintained by quality control. These audits will be recorded and all findings will cause the generation of a QCAR. A report on the audit will be provided to the management of the audited organization. The management of the organization shall engage the QCAR process and take timely action to remedy the finding of nonconformance.

The quality control organization shall consider the organization in nonconformance until a follow up audit has been conducted to verify compliance. The results of the audits and recorded corrective actions taken shall be maintained for a period of five years by quality control.

Note: the establishment of a departmental "Mini Internal Audit (MIA) teams" are encouraged and considered a valuable tool for assessment and improvement of your operations. However, the use of an MIA is not considered sufficient to meet the requirement of this standard and is purely a policy decision by each organization and not to be subjected to audit or full ISO 9000 audit requirements.

Section: 4.18	Date Issued:	
Element: **Training**		
Revision:	Authorized By:	Approved By:

4.18 Training

4.18.1 Scope

All employees who affect quality will require appropriate training and support records. Each organization shall establish and maintain documented procedures for the identification of training needs. Personnel performing these tasks shall be qualified on the basis of education, training, and experience.

The personnel department shall establish procedures for the identification of training requirements. Those departments where the employees reside shall maintain the training record. No employee shall perform a task unassisted until they have been reviewed and their training record indicates successful completion of training to the defined task.

Section: **4.19**	Date Issued:
Element: **Servicing**	
Revision:	Authorized By:	Approved By:

4.19 Servicing

4.19.1 Scope

The service organization shall establish and maintain documented procedures and records as related to the services provided. The servicing procedures shall ensure that a tracking and reporting system is in place to assure that all requirements are met.

The service organization shall ensure that it complies with all other appropriate areas cited within the ISO 90001 standard as it affects their organization. It should be made clear to all service personnel that they shall not work on equipment for which they have not been trained.

The service organization will collect product failure data as defined in the CAR process managed by the sales operations.

Section: 4.20	Date Issued:
Element: Statistical Techniques	
Revision: Authorized By:	Approved By:

4.20 Statistical Techniques

4.20.1 Identification of Need

Each organization will review their operations for opportunities to apply statistical tools for the purpose of improving the capabilities of their processes and product performances. This review will be conducted by the supervision of each area on an annual basis, with a report and plan submitted to quality control, for review by senior management. This report shall include resource requirements such that appropriate resource allocation decisions can be made to maximize the return on investment to the organization.

4.20.2 Procedures

Each organization shall establish and maintain documented procedures to implement and control the applications of statistical techniques. These procedures shall be established in conjunction with the quality control organization and will require QC's approval on the procedures.

Appendix 3

For More Information

Quality Improvement Programs and ISO 9000 Training
Qualtec Quality Services, Inc.
Phone: 407-775-8300   Fax: 407-775-8301
Contact: Bob Ricker

ISO 9000 News and Directory of Registrars and Registered Companies
Quality Systems Update
Phone: 703-250-5900   Fax: 703-250-5313

Foxboro's ISO 9000 Registrar
Det Norske Veritas
Phone: 713-579-9003   Fax: 713-579-1360

For Official Copies of the ISO 9000 Standard and Support Documents
ASQC
Phone: 414-272-8575   Fax: 414-272-1734

To Reach The Authors

John T. Rabbitt	Peter A. Bergh
The Foxboro Company	The Foxboro Company
M.S. N05-3A	M.S. B51-1D
33 Commercial St.	33 Commercial St.
Foxboro, MA 02035	Foxboro, MA 02035

Phone:	508-549-2985	Phone:	508-549-2570
or	508-582-4922	Email:	bergh_peter@foxboro.com
Fax:	508-549-4639	Fax:	508-549-4469

Quality Manual on Disk
If you would like to receive a disk copy of *The Global Competitor's Sample Quality Manual* and *The Thou Shalt According to ISO 9000 Checklist* (MS Word and text format, Windows/DOS or Macintosh) please send a check for $25, made out to LEAF (Lunenburg Educational Advancement Foundation), to LEAF, P. O. Box 1733, Lunenburg, MA 01462, Phone/Fax (508) 582-4922. If you would like to be billed, the price will be $35.

Index

Handling of products *(continued)*
readiness for audit of, 157, 160,
164-165, 168

Historical development
of ISO 9000, 31
of manufacturing, 1-6

I

Identification of products, 19, 133
customer expectations on, 15
on inspection and test status. *See*
Inspection and test status
in quality manual, 185
readiness for audit of, 150, 158, 161,
164, 166
Industry Week Top Ten Award, for
Foxboro Company, 75
Inspection and test status, 16, 19, 138
customer expectations on, 16
deficiencies in, 117
in quality manual, 191
readiness for audit of, 156, 159, 163,
164, 167
Inspection and testing, 19, 123,
135-136
customer expectations on, 16
deficiencies in, 117
documentation of, 135
in emergency situation, 135
equipment in, 16, 19, 136-138
deficiencies of, 117, 123
in quality manual, 189-190
readiness for audit of, 151, 153, 159,
162-163, 166-167
final, 10, 136
in-process, 135-136
of incoming products, 135
in quality manual, 187-188
readiness for audit of, 151, 153,
159, 161-164, 166
status of product concerning. *See*
Inspection and test status
Installation standards, 10, 12
Internal quality audits. *See* Audits,
internal
Introduction to company, in quality
manual, 172

Inventory reduction, 69, 70
Invoices, 59
ISO 9001 standard, 11
activities included in, 10, 12
certification of Foxboro Company
to, 47-78
ISO 9002 standard, 10, 11, 12
ISO 9003 standard, 10, 11, 12
ISO 9004 standard, 9, 11

J

Japan, manufacturing strategies in, 4-5,
6
Just In Time systems, 3, 5, 60, 61

K

Kaiser-Frazer auto company, 4
Kanban systems, 3, 5

L

Lead times, reduction of, 58
Leadership
in ISO 9000 and Baldrige Award, 25,
26
in ISO 9000 and Shingo Prize, 27
Liability for products
European standards on, 35-36
from noncertified suppliers, 37-38
Life-cycle cost of product, 59

M

Management, 25, 26, 27
commitment to ISO 9000
compliance, 21, 83-84
by fact, in Quality Improvement
Process (QIP), 54
readiness for audit of, 145-147
Management representative, designation
of, 126-127
Management responsibility, 18, 21,
125-127, 145-146
customer expectations on, 14
deficiencies in, 117

DATE DUE

DATE DUE			
MAR 2 0 1996			
OCT 0 9 1996			
MAR 0 2 1997			
GAYLORD			PRINTED IN U.S.A